Praise for the Book

Sunil Robert's "Bound to Rise" is a short but wise book, filled with thoughtful guidance for young people trying to steer their careers through a turbulent corporate world. I encourage young professionals everywhere to read it. It has the potential to change the way you think, and even more importantly, the way you act. That is its value.

Mukul Pandya
Executive Director/Editor-in-chief, Knowledge@Wharton

Vision without an Implementation is simply a Hallucination. Likewise a book without an experience that can transform you is just an illusion. Rarely you find someone like Sunil ....; Enjoy this exciting book for your own success with integrity;

Dr. Bala Balachandran
J.L. Kellogg Distinguished Professor of Accounting and Information Management
Northwestern University, Evanston, IL. USA

BOUND TO RISE

Radical Ideas for the
New Corporate World

Sunil Robert

Westland Ltd

westland ltd

61 Silverline Building, 2nd floor, Alapakkam Main Road, Maduravoyal, Chennai 600095
No. 38/10 (New No.5), Raghava Nagar, New Timber Yard Layout, Bangalore 560026
93, 1st Floor, Sham Lal Road, New Delhi 110002

First published in India in westland ltd 2013
Copyright © by Sunil Robert 2013

ISBN: 978-93-83260-11-9

Typeset by Ram Das Lal

Contents

Introduction

Ideas govern the world or throw it into chaos.

– August Comte, French Philosopher

You are a prisoner. I am one too. We are in fetters, of the theories that we hold dear. We are enslaved by the notions that drive us. Our convictions chain us in space and time. We are prisoners of our paradigms. We toss around terms like "Narrow minded" and "Broad minded" when we refer to people whose views are either restrictive or expansive, depending on our own view, often oblivious to the fact, that we are making a value judgement based on our standpoint.

So how do we "jailbreak" from this condition? In the words of a Guru, "You shall know the truth and the truth shall set you free." New ideas always trump archaic ideas. Old-fashioned ideas that have run their course will inevitably be replaced by relevant and compelling ideas.

It has become fashionable to say that we are liberals and freethinkers who believe in intellectual freedom. Fine... but how many of us have an open mind that is not bound by the constraints of habit and conditioning such that we really have the freedom to soar? Let me illustrate and get this across with a retelling of an old story that is relevant even today – Plato's 'Allegory of the Cave'.

Plato's World View

In a deep, dark cave, several men had been kept chained since childhood and knew nothing of the outside world. They could not move their arms, legs or head, and were forced to stare at the wall in front of them. Behind the prisoners was an enormous fire and between the fire and the prisoners was a pathway along which people came and went carrying things on their head including figures of men and animals made of wood, stone and other materials, while the echoes of the noises they made bounced off the walls.

The prisoners avidly observed the shadows cast by the passers-by behind them, and listened to the echoes. They thought these were real and not just reflections of reality, for that was all they had ever seen or heard. They praised whoever could predict which shadow would come next as one who understood the nature of the world, for their lives and their little community were in some way dependent on the shadows that drifted across the wall.

Then, one day, a prisoner shook himself free of his chains, and when he turned around he saw the people and things that had cast the shadows. But he could not recognise them for what they were, and still believed that the shadows they cast on the wall were the real thing. Moreover, the brightness of the fire hurt his eyes and at first, he turned his gaze back towards the shadows. Eventually, he stumbled out of the darkness of the cave into the world outside, full of sunshine and vibrant colours and sounds. But at first, he was distressed because he could not see his 'reality', that is, the shadows on the wall.

After a while however, the freed prisoner acclimatised himself to his new surroundings, until he could look upon and relate to everything around him and understood that this was real. He remembered his first home and what had passed for wisdom there. Then he thought of his fellow prisoners in the cave, the pathetic lives they led and their practice of heaping praise on whoever was best at the game of guessing the progression of the shadows. He pitied them and returned to the cave to share his experiences so as to set them free by showing them the way out of the cave. But when he went back, he found that he was no longer good at their old game for he was no longer accustomed to the darkness. And it was said of him that he had left the cave and returned with his eyes corrupted. So no one wanted to listen to him or follow in his footsteps, for they considered his ideas too dangerous and subversive. In fact, had they been free, they would have killed the man who had tried to release them from their bondage!

* * *

Three ideas strike me when I read Plato's allegory – that we are bound, that we need to constantly search for freedom from the fetters that bind us, and we need to rise beyond the constraints of our conditioning and learn to view the world from a perspective that is not just liberating, but enriching as well.

After having spent twenty-five years in the corporate world spanning India, UK and the USA, it is my strong belief, backed by empirical evidence that the time has come for new paradigms to be applied to ourselves – we need to change the way we think and act, for there are still too many 'prisoners' who stubbornly choose to remain in 'caves' of their own making. Surely, there ought to be more to life and work than what we often experience!

Many of us have bought into myths that have bred disillusionment and frustration. So, like the prisoners in Plato's allegory should we be condemned to remain in chains? Or, like Sisyphus, are we destined to roll a huge rock up a hill each morning only to watch it roll down again, and be forced to repeat this endless and monotonous charade till we die? I for one, am convinced that we are not born to shoulder the burden of such drudgery.

Using Plato's allegory of the cave as a metaphor, let us explore a few paradigm shifts that will set you free. From endless monotony, you will discover meaning. From bewilderment, you will find clarity. And from dissatisfaction, I am confident you will discover contentment.

What I have attempted through this book is to demonstrate how we have allowed ourselves to remain in bondage to the dictates of a few paradigms that dominate today's workplace when freedom is within our grasp.

Release yourself from these paradigms and I believe you will truly 'rise', and find your experience uplifting because of the discoveries you will make along the way – of a new framework, of a set of ideas that will challenge your past beliefs and enrich your life in ways that you cannot imagine until you learn to step out of your 'cave'.

Each chapter takes you back to Plato's cave only to show you how to break free from a dominant assumption or erroneous but widely held set of notions. What I propose has been tried and tested not only through the prism of my personal experience but by scores of others who have validated these ideas.

So welcome, denizens of the 'cave', for together we shall find a way out into the light!

CHAPTER 1

From Combat to Calling

We are different, in essence, from other men. If you want to win something, run 100 metres. If you want to experience something, run a marathon.

— Emil Zatopek, Czech long-distance runner and
winner of four Olympic gold medals

It started off as a crazy thought. But in November 2009, drawing inspiration from my CEO who had just run the New York City marathon, I decided to run the Philadelphia City half marathon. Later in 2011, I went a step further and also completed the New York City marathon, one of the most challenging courses on the world marathon circuit. From the time I first started training to run the marathon, the lessons that I learnt and the parallels I drew gradually strengthened my conviction that the marathon is a compelling metaphor for our arduous corporate life. It was a discovery that was too momentous to keep to myself, and I felt I had to share it with others.

The Marathon Mindset

The first lesson I learnt was that anyone who wants to run a marathon must re-programme his or her thought processes and attitude. Believe it or not, a marathon mindset is a sporting, yet intense mindset that allows us to focus on finishing well rather than 'winning' the race. That is not as preposterous a concept as our conditioning might lead us to believe, for being a winner is about much more than just coming first. Ask any marathoner, and you will be told that the key is to relax your body, put your mind at ease, and keep running. But most important of all, it is enjoying what you do. Likewise, the key to success both in the corporate world and in life is to do well by staying united with the others around you in a spirit of comradeship and enjoying the run.

This takes me back to a strange incident that took place when I was in danger of losing steam during the New York Marathon. Just a few yards before the Queensboro Bridge, probably the toughest part of the course, I was slowing down to a walk. 'You don't want to slow down here,' said a voice that was loud and clear enough to penetrate my ears even with my iPod earphones in them. I turned and saw a beautiful woman striding alongside me. 'The bridge is just around the corner. Come with me.', she said with a smile. Till we crossed the bridge, she kept pace with me, and then she raced ahead. We had never met and it is unlikely that we shall ever meet again, but that little act of extending moral support to someone competing in the same race epitomises the true spirit of a marathon runner. Everyone who crosses the finish line is a winner. Till then we are all fellow cheerleaders!

A marathon mindset will not only make you successful but also bring meaning, joy and contentment by defining many aspects of your life. You do not look at everything from the perspective of whether you're winning or losing, but imagine that you are running alongside others in the larger race of life. Only in a marathon does a fellow runner egg you to keep going.

In a world that places utmost emphasis on winning, even if it is by trampling over others, can running the race really be as important as winning, if not more so? And will such a 'paced' approach – that is, a long-term view of your work – help you achieve your goals at all?

Look at it this way. Such a shift in your perspective would radically reposition you for long-term success without your ending up all frazzled and burnt-out in a hyper-competitive environment. Can't imagine how that is possible? Well, believe me, it is! My own life is a powerful affirmation of this. Through the pages of this book, I shall be sharing with you the secret of living life holistically on your terms, holding your own and actually emerging a winner even in the frenetic environment of today, without losing your mind or your health.

I have distilled more than twenty years of work experience all over the world to offer this alternative, for work was never meant to be a drudgery. It ought to be a compelling expression of all that you are passionate about and a true reflection of yourself. In this chapter, we shall be looking at what the marathon mindset is all about, and later go on to explore why it is unique and how you can adapt it not just to add a special dimension to your life but to change it altogether... and emerge from your 'cave'. So what are some of the unexpected discoveries you will make when you go for that paradigm shift from a sprinter's mindset to that of a marathon runner? Here's an overview...

The USP of the Marathon Mindset

A person with a marathon mindset is someone who is acutely aware of his calling and driven by it. A competitive person goes a long way, but a person with a calling goes the full distance. If you keep this in mind and consciously change your attitude, you will go places, build more friendships along the way and make work (or whatever it is that you undertake) a delightful experience. As we all know, it was the joy of conveying good news and not the act of outrunning a competitor that spurred the runner Pheidippides in 490 BC, to run from the battlefield of Marathon to the City of Athens, covering a distance of twenty-five miles, after the Athenians, with the Spartans as allies, emerged victorious against the attacking Persian army.

Life Is More Than a Win-Lose Battle

A competitive mindset presumes a win-lose equation. One needs to out-manoeuvre, outsmart and defeat an opponent in order to win a competition. In a marathon, you focus more on yourself rather than on your competitors. Except maybe in the case of elite athletes, long-distance runners are usually pitted against themselves. The ruthlessness associated with the competitive mindset, which makes one try to get the better of others at any cost, stems from the belief that the spoils are few and there are many players. So what do you do if you find yourself in such a situation, say, at your workplace? Well, you give yourself the permission to rewrite the rules of the game and go with what you are comfortable. Let me put this across differently. Ask yourself the question: 'How many years am I going to remain a corporate executive?' If the answer is in double digits, then you'll have enough opportunities to shine and cover yourself in glory without resorting to anything that you would not be proud of later on. If the answer is less than that, surely you would not wish to wrap up your career with something that weighs heavily on your conscience!

Now to get to the crux of the matter – why is the corporate setting so vicious and ruthless? Despite all the talk of fairness and values, why is it that a sense of injustice and distrust pervades the workplace? Often, there is a lot of unfair competition and the rules of the game are not clearly defined. Sometimes, your own impatience to get to the top is to blame, along with unreasonable goals that cannot be accomplished, or at least not in the timeframe you envisage and this leads to dejection and anger. Remember, it is a law of nature that the cream rises to the top, but you have to keep churning the milk. There is constant pressure on everyone to play better than everyone else, which creates stress because someone's victory is at the cost of another's downfall, because of the 'zero sum game' that the corporate world makes it out to be. As a result, there is politicking and shadow boxing, which vitiates the ambience and culture of the teams.

On the other hand, the marathon mindset lets people play according to their own rhythm and pace. Because they are focused on performing at their best, they do not indulge in the pernicious game of comparisons which invariably leads to resentment. So if you take a deep breath and a long-term view of your life and priorities, you will experience a sense of liberation that will not just free you from such hurtful negative feelings but enrich your personal life as well.

You Can Make Your Own Rules

What exactly can you expect if you cultivate the marathon mindset? First, you will find that you are marching to your own heartbeat, so while everyone is making a dash for the short-term spoils, you are not sucked into that game. As a result, it will be easier for you to define your rules of engagement and get around those who want to control you. Sure, you are willing to listen and engage with others, but you will find that you are in a situation that allows you to play the game by your rules. Maybe, when you are young and still learning, the organisation might keep you on a tight leash and you might not be allowed to take very many liberties at your workplace, but you could make sure that your voice is heard when you speak your mind. How? Being a skilled communicator is the key to that – it allows you to be your own person in the face of keen competition. And being a functionally dextrous player is an add-on card!

'Yes, I've Had Instant Success – Only Thing, It Took Me a Few Decades!'

You now know that the marathoner is focused on the long haul while the competitive player wants to win every game. The ferocity of ambition pervades every move, and permeates every word, every choice at work, and the player is driven by a win-it-all-at-any-cost mindset even while chasing minor short-term aims. There is no sense of belonging to any team, or organisation, and the only loyalty the player has is towards himself, and his only incentives are the rewards he hopes to reap. Often, starry-eyed young graduates from top schools enter the business world, burning bright with ambition and dreams of instant success. While their confidence and skills are a force to reckon with, what they are short of are patience and tact. So inevitably, they have a run-in with old-timers who consider themselves pillars of the organisation. Pretty soon, they ruffle enough feathers to make their work environment uncomfortable, just because they have not taken the time to understand the dynamics of the organisation. Whenever you join a new team, organisation or environment, wait till things settle down and the equilibrium is re-established. If you make a move even before the ripples settle in the pond, you are setting yourself up to face a lot of churning and turbulence in the waters.

There is an anecdote about a young man in New York City who approached an elderly person on the street and asked, 'How do I get to Carnegie Hall?' and got the answer, 'A lifetime of practice, son!' So instead of obsessing about winning NOW, this very instant, take your time to run the corporate race and learn to enjoy what you do. You'll not only finish, but finish strong, and have fun along the way.

When a winner-takes-all mindset dominates the workplace, everyone fights hard to conquer and grab the spoils by 'defeating' their colleagues. This often results in bickering, office politics, vendettas and turf wars. Once you are freed from such a mindset, you will be playing equally hard but after rewriting the rules of the game. You are still hungry for success, but your aim is to free yourself to claim greater glory and the big prize. A marathon mindset liberates you from the constant need for immediate gratification.

Caring Companions Outrun Blustering Bullies

Rather than being admired for their dynamism, those who are overly competitive and aggressive at the workplace – whether they are co-workers or even your superiors – leave a negative impression, because interacting with them leads to unpleasantness. These powerful people simply bully others into submission, often in a disrespectful manner, and kindle deep-rooted resentment, envy, anger and frustration because they make others feel used or abused, even as they continue to harvest rewards and riches. When such bitter feelings are constantly evoked, the tables could eventually turn and the 'bully' might find himself in a nightmare of his own making. In a corporate setting sooner or later, power equations change. So if you are as good as you believe you are and make the effort to build relationships instead of tearing down people, you'll find your place under the sun. On your own terms. Watch your behaviour and communication style closely. If you are throwing rank constantly at others, it indicates that you are leading by designation, not by influence. People skills are therefore critical.

Run a Marathon: Multiply Your Life Skills

Twelve years ago I was in a serious motorbike accident in Hyderabad that put my right leg out of action and left me completely incapacitated. Although with surgery I was able to walk again, my leg was nowhere near normal, and whether I was swimming or jogging I had to bear in mind that I had a partial handicap, and work around it. During some medical tests, I also discovered that I was suffering from high blood pressure. With a genetic history of heart problems, I found myself sliding towards trouble. Either I could blame my knee injury and make excuses to sit back and do nothing, or take control of my health. I was still undecided as to what I should do when a talk by my CEO, who had taken to running in his early forties, spurred me to action – and how! Initially, I took baby steps. Then within three or four months, I evolved into a long-distance runner who could do a twelve-minute mile. And, along the way, I picked up a host of life skills such as these...

How to Manage Time Effectively

Measure Everything

Running is a sport that could come close to self-inflicted torture if you don't learn to love it. And as I ran, I began to engage in absorbing conversations with myself. Soon, I found that running and life were strikingly similar. If you want to be even a casual long-distance runner – assuming that there is such a thing! – you need to measure everything. Similarly, in time management (which is imperative for success whether you're a homemaker or the CEO of a company), the first step is to measure everything. 'What you cannot measure, you cannot monitor,' is a popular adage in the corporate world and I got to appreciate this better after I took up running. When you run, you measure the time to warm-up, you measure your first mile, and you measure the time you start winding down. There are runners who quantify and analyse their race time, mile by mile, just so that they can measure where they did well and where they slackened, in order to gain a comprehensive view of how their body behaved during the entire course of the race.

Time Management Is Resource Management

Another invaluable lesson that I learnt was that time management was resource management. In the early months of my training when I could barely stay on the treadmill for five minutes, enhancing my stamina so that I could last on the machine for a full hour became my first goal. Actually, it didn't matter whether I worked out on the treadmill or ran on the road – I just had to accomplish that! Initially, I was able to jog for three miles but as my knees gained strength I was able to increase the distance.

Goals are the 'milestones' for a runner. Likewise, if you want to make a mark in the corporate world, you need to plot your milestones and how you are going to reach them, down to the smallest detail possible. What started off as a crazy thought when I heard a speech by my CEO became a serious goal for me after I ran the Philadelphia City half marathon. I decided to run a full marathon, planned and worked hard and accomplished my goal. And no value can be placed on my reduced blood pressure, quality of life, and the inspiration I was able to provide to friends and family just by setting those goals.

So what are your goals? Professionally, aside from your work goals, do you constantly aspire to excel in your chosen area? Do you set targets to improve yourself? Do you set financial goals? Because your time management is eventually governed by your goals. Life management is nothing but combining your goals and resources. If you are not driven by enough goals, then you will look back and wonder what happened to you during the weeks that went by. Sadly, some people even let years go by before they wake up wondering what they've accomplished. Impoverished is the person who has let time go by. It was Benjamin Franklin who said, 'Young man, dost thou love life, squander not time, for this is the stuff life is made of.'

Pacing yourself is critical, in life as well as in long-distance running. If you are always running high on adrenaline and not slowing down, you are setting yourself up for a burn-out, if not a breakdown. There are times when you have to dig deep into your inner reservoir and give it all you've got, but mostly, you need to regulate how you expend your energy. Proper pacing is the secret of sustaining yourself over the long haul, without getting enervated.

The other side of pacing is planning. Only when you know in your mind's eye when to turn up the energy, will you be able to brace yourself and commit to that burst of activity. Once I started training for my half marathon, I realised that the only way I could last the course was by breaking it up into smaller segments, and by pacing myself. There are moments in the race when you have to take it one step and one stride at a time. There are moments when you run uphill and you have to put your best foot forward. But when you are running downhill, you can recoup your energies by easing up a bit.

Similarly, the best way to finish a long task or a huge project is to break it down into milestones. Not all of us may be project managers but if you consider the full scope of your life, each area is like a project. You might be appearing for a competitive examination, or organising something big, say, a wedding in the family. You can save yourself a lot of stress by meticulously planning the whole event in detail so that no time is wasted during its execution; and then, working at it one step at a time.

'Seize the minute and you'll pretty soon have captured an hour,' as the saying goes. If you can discipline yourself not to fritter away minutes, you will be amazed at how much more you can pack into your life. Even a decision to not plan is a decision – it means you chose to merely respond to events and let life come at you. Sure there are life-defining events that happen, like a sickness or a sudden crisis that might derail your schedule. But barring those extraordinary events, if you have not planned your life well, your time – that most precious commodity – will be wasted... lost forever. Ask any achiever. The secret formula behind their success is the way they use their time, for they train longer and harder when others give up... Champions are not made in the ring; they are merely showcased there. Their battles are won during the mundane, boring routine of daily tasks.

How to Take on Larger-Than-Life Goals and Succeed

This is not as mind-boggling as it seems. Begin at the beginning with GOAL.

- **Go:** Where you want to go should be significantly further away from where you are at now. Think hard: what are your current challenges and opportunities? What is the most compelling desire that needs to be achieved?
- **Observe Current Reality:** What are the difficulties that need to be overcome? What's not working?
- **Assess:** What's missing? Stand inside the gap between vision and reality. Assess what's lacking, which, if attained, could make a difference.

- **Learn and Improve:** You need to think fast as your plans unfold. Keep in mind the motto: fail frequently, learn fast. If you don't make course corrections, you'll go further away from where you wish to be, making the comeback that much more difficult.

Each year, I set goals for myself and my family that encompass multiple aspects of my life. Some get done right away but some take longer, and some probably will never get done in a hurry. But since I constantly have those goals at the back of my mind, it is hard for anyone or anything to distract me from my mission.

How to Handle Disappointments and Fight Jealousy and Insecurity

Since the marathon runner is not worried about short-term losses simply because he focuses on the final outcome, it makes it easier for him to cope when things do not go his way. But how does it translate in a day-to-day context, at the workplace? Well, a bad appraisal, or a bad boss, for instance, is seen as a temporary hurdle rather than a perennial problem, and once you learn to look at things from a broader perspective, life becomes far less stressful, and you do not allow your energy to be channelled in negative ways.

The marathon runner is also able to whole-heartedly applaud others. He recognises that the task ahead is a task of endurance and not necessarily one of overpowering his competitors. Similarly, in a corporate environment, if you are able to recognise and appreciate others who perform well instead of seething with envy, such an outlook will certainly help you build relationships and keep your stress levels down.

Trade Old Accolades for New Challenges

One of the hardest lessons a marathon runner learns is that he needs to move on from his crowning moments and reinvent himself regularly. This is equally relevant in a corporate setting, especially now that we are living in an age of rapid skill obsolescence. Any movement, lateral or vertical enables us to grow and expand our skills. Over the past two decades, I have had to keep upgrading myself with newer skills while expanding my knowledge horizons to embrace new opportunities. Whether it was ditching my electronics background to try something else, or moving to new cities or new countries, my journey was that much richer because I was willing to trade in my old accolades for new challenges.

Tips to Combat Insecurity and Jealousy

- Redefine your goals independent of corporate annual appraisals or peer measurements.
- Try to be graceful and celebrate others' victories without snide or sarcastic remarks.
- If you've worked hard and given it your best, take pride in your signature work.
- Have goals and avocations outside of work, which can give you a sense of balance and perspective.

So What Are the Benefits You Reap?

Once you learn to handle disappointments and are rid of insecurity, jealousy and the consequent negativity that has been dragging you down, you will find peace of mind and be able to tackle your tasks, interact with others and reinvent yourself to meet new challenges with renewed energy. This is essential because the corporate world is in a state of flux and, as mentioned earlier, skill obsolescence has now become a fact of life. With the advent of New Age technologies and globalisation, it has become incumbent on the workforce around the world to keep abreast of the changes that are happening everywhere.

Once people settle into their comfort zone, learning slows down and the Peter Principle kicks in: *each one rises to his own level of incompetence.* In other words, if you are not a constant learner, you stagnate and stop growing. One of the reasons some seniors don't let others grow in the organisation is because of their own inability to take on new responsibilities and grow. Hence, our ability to keep our mind open to change, so as to reinvent ourselves regularly is an important asset.

Combatants versus Runners

A marathon runner has a clear map of the course and a well-thought-out strategy. He floats, paces himself or plods on, depending on the stretch that he is navigating. Likewise, to function effectively in the competitive and often manipulative environment of the corporate world, you need a clear vision of the course and a carefully calibrated plan of action. There is no point in crawling across the finish line, beaten, bruised and bloodied. The key to success both in the corporate world and in life is to do well by enjoying the run. In other words: do what you enjoy, and enjoy what you do! How? Trade in your old trophies, seek out new challenges and reinvent yourself to conquer them.

Are you ready for the metamorphosis?

CHAPTER 2

From Racing to Reinventing

"What brought you here, won't take you to the next station"

Smart Strategies to Reinvent Yourself

Like the men in Plato's allegory, most people dread any change, big or small. But the marathon runner's tried and trusted strategies will help you reinvent yourself pretty painlessly, to meet the world on your terms. So get set to welcome the unexpected and embrace the new you!

Why Should You Reinvent Yourself?

Whether you look at a superstar in the world of sport, or even in the most ruthless of all industries – the entertainment world – those who are constantly reinventing themselves are the ones who are most successful. Whether it is Madonna in the music world, or our very own Amitabh Bachchan, look at the way they keep coming back in new avatars all the time!

When Should You Reinvent Yourself?

Yesterday, today, tomorrow... the time is always right for this! The biggest tragedy in the world is the tragedy of a wasted life, and the saddest last words are: 'If only...' Often, people wait a lifetime for the right opportunity to come by, only to discover that it is too late for them to do anything. It is better by far to take a shot at every opportunity that comes your way and make the best of it. You might fail at times but you would not have allowed something with the potential to transform your life, slip away unheeded.

Reinvent When You Hit a Plateau: Ask yourself honestly, 'Does my job or work excite me enough to make me jump out of bed every morning, or would I much rather do something else?' True, there are times when you feel you need to hang on to the lucrative job that you have no matter how dissatisfied you might be with it, so as to support your lifestyle or the needs of your family. But if you hate your job, you could be called upon to pay a heavy price for clinging to it, for it could take a toll on you physically and emotionally. Ask yourself if it is worth the pain you are in. Would it not be worthwhile to get out of your comfort zone and make the adjustments necessary for leading a fuller life? Surely, you can explore ways of dividing your responsibilities with your spouse or parents, or downsizing your lifestyle for a while. Life is short; enjoy it while you work. It's time to shake yourself out of your lethargy and explore what lies outside the rut you think you are happy wallowing in.

Reinvent When You Feel Underwhelmed: More and more frequently, while at work, have you begun to tell yourself, 'This is not what I am called to do'? Does your job leave you totally underwhelmed, and do you feel it can be done by a rookie or someone with half your skills or experience? When you assess your work honestly, ruthlessly, do you find there is nothing special or unusual that you bring to the table? If so, the chances are that you are doing something that either does not utilise your full potential or enrich you in any way. You are operating below par, and it would be a good time to reinvent yourself and find your zone where you can make full use of your abilities.

Reinvent When You Are Overwhelmed: During the early days of my career, I often returned home completely overwhelmed because I felt my education and training were inadequate for the job I was doing. While I was quick to rebound from failure partly because I had no choice, I carried that cloud of despair around me for a long time, waiting desperately for a shower of success to dispel the gloom. Sometimes, we are in jobs that are either too big for us, or we have taken on too much and that adds to our sense of inadequacy. Again, in such situations, you may need to reinvent yourself. Only when I quit engineering sales to get into advertising did I find the right spot for myself.

Reinvent to Ride the Wave of Emerging Opportunities: You don't have to consult fortune-tellers to read your future, or even the future of your industry. If you are clued in on the happenings around you, you'll have a pretty good idea of what is around the corner. Have you made sure that you are in the right position to ride the next wave of opportunities? Or do you usually find yourself at the end of a long queue when something crucial opens up? Are you always out when opportunity knocks, and then, when you're all set to surge ahead, do those once-in-a-lifetime chances seem to dry up and leave you seething with frustration? Take a good hard look at what you want, hone your radar so that you're alerted whenever there is something worthwhile, then go grab those chances!

A few years ago, I mentored a friend who was cut out to be an entrepreneur. After a long period of doing all the right things – branding, sales calls, putting in long hours at work – she ran out of patience, wound up shop, and took an overseas flight back home. Exactly twenty-four hours later, the largest multinational in the city called to offer her a contract that she had pursued with vigour. If only she had waited a few more hours, her dream of becoming a successful entrepreneur would have come true.

Reinvent to Suit Yourself: Before you decide to change gears, consider the various dimensions that need to be taken into account. How much gas is there in your tank? What is the price you will have to pay – emotionally, spiritually, physically – and how would it affect your relationships? There is a time to sow, and a time to reap. And only you can answer the question, 'Have I fought the good fight? Have I run the race well?' There are variables in some equations that only you can work out. So go ahead and do it... don't put it off.

What should you do to reinvent yourself?

Step Away from Your Star Performance: Always remember the most important rule of reinvention: those who wish to reinvent themselves must first step away from all their moments of past glory, and constantly be on the lookout for opportunities to grow and enrich themselves. The corporate world is full of folks who rest on their wilting laurels clinging to their rewards for work done in the distant past, forgetting that each day is a new one and that the scorecard starts all over again. So, shrug off any baggage that you might carry even if it comes trailing clouds of glory, start afresh, and aim for the next big wave to ride as that might proffer an opportunity to redefine yourself, once more.

Aim for Visibility in Your Profession: Aim for peer recognition or visibility in the industry. Most professions are governed by industry bodies that offer certification and regular validation of skills through testing. Participate in these – you will be pitted against the best of your fellow practitioners in the industry and you can utilise this opportunity to hone your skills, and also benefit by interacting with the others.

In fact, in the west, it is often imperative that one acquires a certification or a degree in one's chosen profession. And such a certification usually comes with an expiry date. Rightly so! Just because I have a management degree that I acquired ten years ago, it does not mean that I am on top of the game now. Constant learning will encourage you to be a 'fresh' thinker, speaker and practitioner of your trade. So think… when was the last time you acquired a certificate, or when did your work last win you plaudits?

Certification, subscribing to reputed journals that help you glean relevant information and keep you updated on what is happening in your field, and membership of industry bodies are often the magic wands that can open doors in many professional areas. Contributions at industry forums and publishing in the industry media reinforce what you say. Also, when you constantly upgrade yourself, it becomes your safety net and makes it easier for you to take risks – after all, what progress can there be unless you are willing to take calculated risks?

The Difference Between Flitting and Reinventing

Your CV is a narrative and it needs to be a compelling story, with each move that you make tightly meshing with the next one. If your CV reveals inconsistencies, or that you have been flitting from job to job on the flimsiest of pretexts, you will find it difficult to create a favourable impression. And your track record can either haunt you or break open doors for you.

Reinventing yourself means adding more responsibilities, more qualifications, and more variety and range to your job description, not changing jobs for a small jump in salary (which, in fact, could hurt your long-term prospects). When I moved from public relations to analyst relations, I persuaded my boss to send me to seminars that were geared for AR professionals, and even applied for certification. Earlier on, as an aspiring writer, I invested my time and money to attend courses designed for budding writers, knowing full well that I might be able to retain and use only a few of the key ideas that I picked up there. But then, if you are not a committed learner who constantly seeks to excel in what you are doing, you cannot grow as a person. Which is why, if there was an award for professionals in my field, I saw it as a benchmark and measured my performance against those of the recipients who were honoured.

What Happens to the Skills Acquired Earlier On?

Most of the skills that you pick up at an earlier stage provide you with a solid base and serve as stepping stones when you set out to acquire the next level of skills and reinvent yourself. What sets you up for growth and promotions are the deep and wide range of skills that you continue to acquire over a period of time, particularly if you are in a field where the job descriptions are not all that clear cut.

Bear in mind, however, that sometimes the new skills you acquire might not provide you with any significant advantage immediately, as they may have to be used in an altogether new environment. For example, in my own professional journey I discovered that young kids who straightaway took to PR and me, with all the experience I had acquired, were pretty much in the same cluster of job roles because of their fancy degrees. And they had fancy designations to boot, but that did not make me feel insecure. The storms that I had navigated and the experiences that had shaped me over the years had become a valuable part of me. All of these stood me in good stead because I accepted them in the right spirit. In fact, like a marathon runner, I often fed off the energy and ambition of my younger colleagues to galvanise and reinvent myself. And since I brought the experience of sales, advertising and PR into my role as a communicator, I was able to work with some of the finest professionals globally without being overwhelmed. So it all turned out rather well in the end!

Become a Champion Communicator

One of the most important lessons I learnt in my role as a communicator was that you cannot reinvent yourself effectively without fine-tuning your communication skills. Over the years, because I have been working in the area of communications, I have often been asked to share my ideas on what makes a good communicator, as well as the secret of dynamic, impactful communication. I have found that several factors add up to make a good communicator. But first, let me touch upon the flip side of this. We assume that a back-slapping, gregarious, outgoing person must be a good communicator. But I have often found that such people – including myself! – commit the most atrocious *faux pas* because of a strong streak of overconfidence or a desire to play to the gallery. So if you suffer from these failings and repeatedly find yourself in embarrassing or humiliating situations, take time to introspect on the negative feedback that is probably being dished out to you with alarming regularity.

Glib talkers are not necessarily good communicators. Their very strength – that words roll off their tongue with ease – could become a limitation, because they are so caught up in spouting their own opinions that they refuse to see other people's perspectives, and may not be able to reach out to others.

A good communicator is a mature thinker. I know we usually associate the word 'mature' with a bald pate or a wrinkly face, but good communicators are those who possess the uncanny ability to read people. Usually, that comes with years of experience or an intuitive grasp of the human psyche. Good communicators think before they speak; great communicators make sure that each word they utter is carefully calibrated and calculated to carry the precise amount of firepower required for each occasion. They are unlikely to say something off the cuff, because they mentally replay their words many times over before they articulate them.

A good communicator is a good listener. In the hustle and bustle of today's world, people are in such a mad rush that they are in a hurry to talk before they even listen to what the other person is saying let alone think about it, so they do not get down to exploring the touch points essential for building the rapport that is the foundation of good communication. If someone had given me a rupee each time I clicked my tongue and said something dumb, I'd have been a millionaire by now. Of late, even my young son has been making me eat many a thoughtless word of mine spoken without really listening to him, by proving me wrong. Jokingly, I end up saying, 'I like the crunchy sound words make when I eat them.' Or, 'I did not know humble pie tasted so good!'

Good communication is built on the foundation of empathy. I have realised that the more I am focused on the other person, the better the process of communication. Communication is never about you, it is always about your recipient – your target – and the response you desire from the other person, group or audience. Around the world, I have found that there is no weapon more potent than empathy in building relationships. Even in situations where language is a barrier, empathy allows you to make connections. It is hard to describe empathy but if you can role-play yourself into the other person's character, you are getting there. Being so likeminded that you are able to echo and mirror the other person's thoughts is getting close to good communication. That allows you to get to a point when mere gestures or eye contact will facilitate communication.

A good communicator is super-sensitive. Navigating through the maze of domestic or office politics is possible only when you are sensitive to the environment and the reactions of the people involved, for every word, every gesture tends to be scrutinized and interpreted (or misinterpreted). And if you find that it is necessary to point out shortcomings or pull up someone, speak factually and calmly, and in private. Bullying or bulldozing others into submission may work sometimes but it is not a smart strategy for the long haul.

A good communicator asks the right questions. There is no punishment for asking good questions. But Indian corporate culture is such that we feel asking questions might be misconstrued as undermining the person to whom they are addressed. We need to master the art of asking pertinent questions while focusing on the task at hand, for when we ask the right questions, it helps us explore the issues further and clarifies our thoughts. It actually helps everyone because others too might have been grappling with the same difficulties, but may not have felt confident enough to voice them. Plus you connect with everyone else in the picture each time you ask a question or contribute an answer, and this puts you way ahead of those who do not participate actively, say, in meetings or in group discussions.

More Tricks of the Trade

What if you are the sort who breaks into a sweat at the thought of even saying 'Hello' to a group of strangers? Where can you start and how do you go about making allies and influencing friends, colleagues and countrymen?

Begin small. If initially, face-to-face verbal communication seems difficult, whenever possible practise what you wish to say – jot down a few points if you like – and engage with people over the phone. Then, try speaking to others in informal settings. Start with small groups of people with whom you are slightly acquainted. When you do this often enough, you will gain enough confidence to make such interactions a part of your regular routine. Next, pick up a joke or a brief anecdote with a twist and surprise people by narrating it. Again, practise beforehand and choose an informal setting, before you experiment with colleagues at work. Build a strong set of supportive buddies who can egg you on, in the process.

What if you feel you're still not ready to hobnob with others...? Well then, develop your silence as a strong weapon in your arsenal and make it work by supplementing it with other communication tools. I once had a colleague who was by far the shyest person I had ever worked with, but what we churned out as a team was super. Whenever she didn't agree with me, she did not talk about it, but her body language or her nervous laugh told me instantly that I had hit a roadblock, and that I had been trying to bulldoze her into doing things my way, and wasn't going to succeed. With a sigh I would ask her, 'So what is your opinion on this?' And she would invariably reply, 'Let me write you an email.' She hardly ever spoke, but her emails were clear, witty and well thought out, and our email discussions worked just fine!

Communicating effectively with others is a skill that not everyone possesses. In fact, it is very often an acquired skill, and the good news is that anyone – including the meek, the reserved and the painfully shy – can pick it up if they make the effort and persevere, persevere, persevere...

From Ascent to Adventure

Forget the ladder, think roller coaster. Traditionally, life in the professional world is represented by the metaphor of a ladder. But it is one of the most devastating tragedies in life to labour your way to the top of a ladder only to discover that it is leaning against the wrong wall. Forget whether it is leaning against a wall at all... today, the metaphor of the ladder is obsolete. In my experience, those who allow themselves to be guided by it spend a lifetime frantically racing up, and in the process stepping over the very people who labour for their success. As a result, while they go up firmly riding on the shoulders of their colleagues, they leave behind a debris of broken hearts, and a trail of resentful individuals. As a young sports journalist, I interviewed the cricketer, Vinod Kambli who once said, 'Sachin Tendulkar took the elevator, I took the stairs.' Unfortunately, the elevator kept going much higher than the stairs. Ask any cricket pundit to explain the perennial success of the greatest Indian cricketer ever, they will probably tell you that Sachin viewed his game as an adventure to be enjoyed rather than a set of achievements.

The new metaphor that should be embraced is that of a roller coaster, for it will motivate you right from the time you walk into an office with stars in your eyes, or start a firm with a desire to change the world or your own fortunes. While your progress up the ladder can be punctuated by static spells, you cannot complain of a single dull moment on a roller coaster ride. While the nature of your ascent up the ladder might be predictable, you never know what you will encounter while on a roller coaster. So ask yourself this pertinent question: do you think you are on a ladder or are you going topsy-turvy on a roller coaster?

What's extraordinary about the roller coaster is that everyone on the ride experiences a heady thrill. While only folks who are high on the ladder can probably enjoy the view from the top, while the others keep waiting for each rung to be vacated so that they can claw their way up there. Those who adopt the roller coaster view of life are serious risk-takers who are willing to wager on their capabilities, take a bold step, and give themselves wholeheartedly to the ride. The climbers on the ladder are forever scheming, dreaming, waiting and watching for their careers to move to the next level. In today's corporate world, it is highly unlikely that you will make a significant mark, if you take the slow and cautious approach that could cost you a fairly significant chunk of your lifetime, for a place on the next rung. Today, organisations are increasingly looking for individuals who are willing to go beyond their sphere of influence and demonstrate leadership qualities that will stand them in good stead when called on to shoulder new challenges and responsibilities.

There is no pause button for those who are on the roller coaster. For thrill-seekers with a roller coaster mindset, each project, each assignment, each task is a 'ride'. They are not willing to play the waiting game, and are eager to get on with the tasks ahead. They don't like to waste time sitting through mundane meetings. They would much rather keep hacking away at the mountain, no matter how large it seems.

On the other hand, the folks with the ladder mindset like to mull over things and play safe, making sure that their turf is protected, their boss' turf is protected… In the corporate world, the dynamic ones who push for the surge ahead abide by the mantra: seek forgiveness, not permission. They can make things happen, just by asking the right questions and making the right moves. The ladder folks always cover their bases and play in defence, constantly asking themselves the question: Will I be blamed, if something goes wrong? Once they are protected, they breathe a sigh of relief, and only then make their moves.

The ladder folks never trust others and operate from a paradigm of insecurity and fear. The roller coaster folks ride on courage and an appetite for risk-taking, whereas the ladder type executives ensure that they apparently never fail even when they do not succeed. On the other hand, the rollercoaster folks go for broke, and give it their all. They learn to fail and move on taking everything in their stride, and achieve a higher proportion of successes because they are constantly moving from failure to success without being ensnared by either result. If something does not work, they figure out another way by using the experience they acquire through their failure. The ladder people, like the prisoners in Plato's cave, cannot deal with ambiguity and uncertainty, but the roller coaster folks thrive on tackling the unknown. The unknown has a mysterious appeal for them and they are forever delving into the future by painting their dreams with bold brushes.

The ladder folks cling to their positions and power

structures whereas the roller coaster riders are willing to let go of everything from the past, in search of a brand new world. They are willing to relocate, reposition themselves and rewrite their roles for the excitement of a new journey. They are confident that skills can be learnt, tools acquired, and new programmes implemented, so they dive headlong into the vision painted either by themselves or by a leader who is another kindred spirit.

I have mentored a few people along my corporate journey, and those who shine are invariably the ones who are willing to risk everything and plunge into the unknown. Let me share the story of Madhav, who was working in a non-profit organisation helping hundreds of people. From a modest background, he was right in the centre of what, many affirmed, was his calling. He inspired and drew people to him and had a natural propensity for networking and connecting with others. After many years, he felt that he should take a shot at the corporate world, but that would mean going back to level zero on the elevator and moving in a different direction. While his kids were at school, he took a huge loan and went to the UK for a two-year MBA and he is now the COO of a top business group in South India. While he was studying, he was competing with classmates who were many years younger, but his experience and persistence was a valuable factor in his 'success mix'. In the face of intense competition, he managed to come out on top and was named European MBA Student of the Year.

But he did not rest on his laurels. Instead, he decided to

do something different, something he was interested in, so he converted his dorm into a networking hub and his small room into a counsellor's cabin. He was on a rollercoaster, helping friends and classmates, even those who had envied his success. While in the UK, he became a bridge between Indian and Scottish companies, and organised large events for them. Those who competed with him adopted the usual strategies – backbiting, disparaging remarks, negativity and mean-spirited behaviour. But you can never put a good man down. As people discovered that he was the 'real deal' without any pretensions, they slowly rallied around him and supported him in his bold 'adventures'. Madhav was a regular at the pubs, not for the drinks, but because the others felt that no evening was complete without his spirited story-telling. He proved to be a role model to many of his younger classmates who felt disoriented in the highly charged and competitive environment where they had to function. I always take pride in rooting for this underdog, because he strapped himself into a roller coaster and had a different kind of ride, and all of us are richer because of his courage.

It does not mean that these riders do not feel the strong urge to quit, or stay cosy in their comfort zone. It is just that their urge to move closer to their vision is stronger than the desire to stop. For instance, two weeks into his course, as the sheen wore off and the heat was turned on, Madhav had called me and said 'This is clearly not for me. The folks around me are younger, sharper and hungry for success. I am quitting... in fact, I'm about to head for the airport to take the flight back to India.'

I spent a long time chatting with Madhav, explaining the nuances of business school. I reminded him that he had spent his entire life, urging people not to quit but keep fighting in good faith, and it was time for him to practise what he preached. At the end of the call, we made a deal: he would stay in B-school for two more weeks and then, if he still felt strongly about quitting, he could go ahead and do so. I did not hear from him for a long time, and when the phone call came, it was about how excited he was about participating in the European MBA Student of the Year contest, which he went on to win.

Before every roller coaster ride, there is fear in your gut and you feel butterflies flying in your stomach. But those who want to ride know how to make the butterflies fly in a pattern. They know that fear is good and they learn to harness it anyway. Whereas those who opt for the ladder model do not make vastly random moves but take the incremental growth path, one step at a time. With such an approach, you are comfortable holding on to what you have, and only let go to jump to a higher rung whenever the slot becomes free. In the case of a roller coaster rider, it is his fear that propels him. The attraction lies in the danger and such risk-taking, which often brings spectacular returns and failures, only adds to their track record of things attempted.

How do I know this? Well, right from my teens I have veered more towards the roller coaster approach, swinging from job to job, and taking up various avocations, for the thrill of it all. Not one chance did I miss to explore a new opportunity and whether it was the print media, radio, or even television, I kept knocking on various doors. The ladder climbers often spend years on the same rung but I was in a hurry to explore the world, literally and figuratively. And since I could not afford to travel on my own, I needed a job to get me going. As a travelling salesman, I travelled the length and breadth of the country, including some of India's remote industrial areas. And after whetting my appetite, I set my sights overseas and kept moving around till I found an opening in corporate communications and the IT industry, which eventually helped me move abroad. Now, nearly twenty-five years of corporate life have gone by in a blur, and I cannot but look back on the journey with joy. In each country where I have lived, I've engaged in public speaking, travel, and voluntary work while pursuing professional growth. I would not trade my life's experiences for anything else!

Those who choose to get on the roller coaster are not merely risk-takers but are also well-rounded individuals. They discover that they are racing against time and cannot afford the luxury of vertical ascent. So they do not let conventional definitions limit them, rather they go about creating reality based on their dream. They do not let anyone or anything discourage or block them from achieving their goal. If opportunity does not knock on their door, they keep looking out of their window to see if it is beckoning them from some remote corner, to set off on an adventure.

Hallmarks of an Adventurer

Adventurers have a vision of their own. Because they have a purpose and a clear understanding of who they are and what makes them tick, as well as their strengths and weaknesses, they seem to sail through every situation with confidence. Adventurers are so clearly focused on their destination that they even enjoy the minor bumps along the journey.

Adventurers have a signature of their own. These roller coaster riders leave a stamp of distinction on their work. No matter how long or brief their tenure at an organisation, their work bears a unique, personal signature. They stand apart by their sheer zest, commitment and energy. As the years go by, their track record becomes singularly special, so you can expect a certain level of excellence and high quality output, if you have signed on an adventurer. They are always in demand because wherever they go, instead of resting on their past accolades, they contribute fresh inputs. Also, because they have a reputation to protect, they strive to deliver, and that sets in motion a cyclical pattern of continuous expectation.

Adventurers have a brand of their own. While they fit into an organisation like a glove, they always ensure that their personal brand is also built. It is not as if they are mavericks who refuse to be slotted, but they realise the importance of being a brand that carries the label of superior performance. A clear strategy plus conscious brand building takes them to the top… and they enjoy what they do at the workplace! They realise that every brand has a shelf life (as is the case with all products), and it is during that period they need to make themselves relevant and indispensable.

Adventurers have a timing of their own. Everyone in the corporate world comes with an expiration date. Either they move on to bigger things or are assigned to different work areas, but adventurers chalk out their own personal timelines. High performers who are forever chasing a new target, seek to maximise their time. If the project or the work they perform is not compelling enough, they quit or find something that captures their imagination. They encounter failures along the way but even that is seen as a heady learning experience, and they proudly wear it on their resume because it reinforces what they stand for and believe in – the constant search for excellence..

Adventurers have a drive of their own. They work manic hours far beyond what is prescribed by the company simply because they are driven by something that only they understand. Their pulse races and heart pounds at the mere possibility of an exciting project. It has been my personal experience, and it is this elusive elixir that keeps me going. Often, it is the challenge of a seemingly impossible task waiting to be accomplished, which drives me and keeps me going way beyond work, so much so that it becomes a personal issue that just has to be fixed.

But Is It All Worth the Bother?

To put it simply, it is!

Over the past twelve years, I've lived in five cities around the world, changed jobs four times in three countries and have been promoted a few times. While that is not exceptional, what is striking about my own career path is that I constantly kept taking risks. When the advertising industry in Hyderabad hit a rough patch, I moved to Bangalore to ride the tech-growth wave. After spending a couple of years in a large multinational firm, I jumped at the opportunity to move to Mumbai. While at Acer in Bangalore, which was a Taiwanese multinational firm, I was doing fairly well as the brand's very first marketing and communications manager. Rolling out new products at a fast clip for the challenge of taking a small unknown brand to fame appealed to me. There were, however, some fleeting misgivings. What if the plan bombed? What if despite all my plans I did not succeed? Surely, I would be able to get another job because of my Acer experience alone, right...? So with those options, the exhilaration and the anticipation of a new frontier pushed me to take the risk, even if it meant uprooting my family and giving up the comfortable life we had built. I tamed the butterflies in my stomach and took a leap of faith. We moved, started all over again and within three years the Mumbai job had come to an end but not before a heady ride that set me up on a growth trajectory overseas.

Successful people never have to give explanations and

losers cannot afford to give explanations. You don't have to explain success to anybody and nobody will buy an explanation for failure. That is the joy of risk taking. Risk takers know that not taking a risk is suicidal. Surely you'll win some and lose some, but that is a precondition that allows you to jump in with a certain degree of confidence.

When a couple of overseas opportunities came my way, I took what was perceived as a detour to my final destination, but this actually enriched my resume. Going into new 'discomfort zones' helped me polish my language skills. I never let a year pass without constantly challenging myself and exploring various cultural and professional avenues, and my involvement in these areas expanded at each stage. The line between the judicious risk taker and the compulsive gambler is a fine one, and very few know the difference. If you are firmly grounded, hopefully, you will not take irrational risks... unlike the contestant who successfully crossed the one-crore mark in India's most popular game show, *Kaun Banega Crorepati*. It was with the next question for the ultimate five-crore-rupee prize that he hit a roadblock. Since he did not know the answer, the host, Mr. Bachchan, gently hinted that he should withdraw from the game and take the one-crore he was already eligible for in prize money. And so did his parents who were in the audience. At that point, he decided to pray and take his chances... then went on to give the wrong answer and lost the fortune he had won thus far!

To sum up

The metaphors of the ladder and pyramid are slowly losing their relevance for today's knowledge society. Think of the rollercoaster as the new paradigm. There will be moments of inactivity which can be interpreted as waiting times. But the excitement and anticipation far exceeds the time on the knuckle tightening, pulse shattering, and adrenaline exploding high-speed rollercoaster.

CHAPTER 3

From Bonds to Bonding

People will forget what you said, people will forget what you did, but people will never forget how you made them feel.

– Maya Angelou

Relationships need to be painstakingly nurtured, but they are the most rewarding pursuits in Life. Whatever your calling, to be effective it is imperative to fine-tune your people skills. Nothing monumental was ever achieved alone – witness what happened to the enlightened prisoner in Plato's allegory. While your calling propels you forward, it is bonding that gives you the momentum and thrust to climb higher. Only when you are able to rally others around you, or when you put your weight behind others can you ever achieve anything that is significant and lasts a while. The term 'networking' has become a buzzword for this, although it has an impersonal connotation. (Strictly speaking, human beings relate, machines network, but it is now the norm to use the term 'networking' in a human context as well.)

Each human being is unique, and to build a rapport and communicate effectively with others, you need to be aware of their sensibilities, their values, and all that makes them tick. What works with one individual may not click with another simply because the operating factors are different. However, since there are broad behavioural issues at play, which will eventually affect you, it is worth making the effort to understand how human beings relate to one another.

Like the prisoners in Plato's analogy, we are in bonds and fall prey to needless fears until we are able to see the big picture of the people around us. It is bonding with others that makes life meaningful and frees us from the invisible shackles of envy, jealousy and all else that prevent us from rising to our full potential.

How to Network Effectively

1. Be Genuine

'True networking happens when a genuine relationship commences.' Getting attention from someone does not necessarily mean that you have made a connection. For example, take a classroom setting. The most forceful talker or a loud, aggressive bully may make an impression on others, but that does not make him the leader or the most popular kid in class. In fact, the one who is most influential is often not the one who talks the most. So that should put paid to the myth that you need to have a forceful, gregarious personality to be a good networker.

2. Nurture Relationships

Just because you are able to shove a business card into someone's hand and extract one from him or her, doesn't automatically make you acquaintances. In India, people are constantly pushing, jostling or talking to others, but we need to understand that only when two minds meet, or two hearts resonate on a specific issue or topic, will a relationship truly begin. Here, we go about our relationships almost nonchalantly because they happen to us all the time. But relationships are like plants. Just as we tend our seedbeds right from the time the seeds are sown, we ought to go about our relationships with the same mindset and cultivate them over a period of time. In fact, the word 'cultivate' has agrarian connotations in that a farmer or a gardener cultivates his greenery, subjects it to the laws of nature, and waits for the right season to reap his harvest. And so it should be when you network.

3. Learn to Decode Individuals

Everyone has a world view; even Nihilists who believe in nothing have a world view in that they believe in nothing in contrast to others who believe in something. Great relationships happen when we understand each individual and work towards understanding the beliefs and ideas that govern his or her choices and preferences over a period of time.

Do you feel perplexed and frustrated when you run into individuals who seem to put up impenetrable barriers around them? You probably think of them as 'hard nuts to crack' because you cannot understand their world views, which are probably in conflict with yours. But beneath the tough, obstinate exterior, you might find someone who is a perfectly reasonable individual within his or her world view. People make choices consistent with their beliefs and those whose ideas are not in sync with yours are seen as unreasonable or, in extreme cases, even as weirdoes. But how do you deal with a tough boss or colleague who happens to be one such person, and cannot see eye to eye with you? Or perhaps, it's your teenage child who causes you endless heartaches and vice-versa...

One major reason for a breakdown in any relationship could be that you have failed to crack the code – the world view code – of the individual. If only you take the time to decipher and understand his or her persona, you may be able to empathise better with the person. The failure to do so may lead to a relationship crisis. Finally, it boils down to the way we respond to a single question: which is easier to change – your own approach, or someone else's? The answer seems like a self-evident, no-brainer but in our rush, the existential rush to keep moving forward in life, we assume that the world should understand us, whereas true wisdom lies in understanding the world.

So what are the ways in which we can decipher someone's world view? First, find out through what kind of lens does that person look at the world. Is the person an incorrigible optimist, with positive, sunny thoughts, and does he look at everything through rose-tinted spectacles? Or are you dealing with someone who views the world through lens so dark that he almost seems to make a living by spreading misery? The key to building a relationship is to decode the other person's 'meta' view, their big picture of everything under the sun and, sometimes, beyond.

Another crucial element of a person's world view is his understanding or opinion of himself. Some people have such low self-esteem, that one has to dig into a pit deep in the ground in order to relate to them, for they think of themselves as worthless worms and push away anyone who has the capacity to stimulate them. At the other extreme are individuals who are so positive they radiate power and energy, and overwhelm you with their personality. They view themselves as saviours, and right away get down to changing the world, and watch out... that includes you! A healthy individual with a balanced perspective comes somewhere in the middle.

Once you determine what sort of person you are dealing with, you can plan how to relate to him. Recently I had to work with a new colleague who had just joined our organisation. He was a dyed-in-the-wool pessimist with negativity oozing out of the pores of his skin, his emails and his phone calls, although I must admit that his fears were not unfounded. I had to work with him and his team on a project, and that meant coaching him and sometimes pepping him up along the way. Although I was firm and occasionally impatient, I managed to build a rapport with him, and at the end of the project he sent me an effusive thank-you letter. While I'd had to bite my tongue a few times when I felt like lashing out at him, his pessimism had actually alerted us to a dimension that most optimistic people would have missed – covering bases while planning and thinking through all elements that could go wrong. So the trick is to spend time with each individual and build your friendship privately. Sow in private to reap in public. In today's world of communication tools like emails, text messages and social media sites, the distance between thought and thoughtful action is infinitesimal.

Understanding how an individual views others is a key element in building a rapport with someone. Think: Does he embrace other people or does he abhor the very idea of their existence? Jean Paul Sartre reportedly said, 'Hell is other people.' From that we skip to another extreme when we mull over the words of Jesus Christ who said, 'Greater love has no man than one who can lay down his life for a friend'. (Of course, a politician is 'someone who is willing to lay down your life for his sake'!) Every individual is somewhere on that spectrum, and the key to success in relationships is finding where you are and where the other individual may be.

In fact, this understanding determines to what degree your relationship will progress. An individual's perspective of his time, his possessions and willingness to share those precious commodities determine whether he gives to a relationship or takes from it. There is no deeper hurt than the hurt caused by a friend, or someone who violates your trust. Is he the kind of person who values his personal mission more than anything else? Or is he willing to place a premium on relationships? There are many who will pay lip service to such a concept, but there will also be folks who will walk the talk. Making the right judgment is all about picking up cues. Does the individual with whom you are trying to build a relationship view you as an end or a means to an end? That pivotal question will determine how far the relationship will go, for there will be many who would like the benefits of your friendship without paying the price of commitment. In the final analysis, you will know how to gauge a relationship by not only what you invest in it but by the conscious contribution that the other person is willing to make to help you or your cause.

Once you decode the individual, you can find the right way to go about building a relationship. Some of the key steps that need to be borne in mind are:

Range: Who are the people that truly can contribute to your life and your life's mission? You will need 'professional influencers', personal mentors and persuasive relationships to build your circle of relationships. Each relationship is driven by a different dynamic and you need to learn to manage them accordingly.

You may have thousands of acquaintances, but you'll have the time and resources to manage only a few significant relationships. The range depends on the stage of your career, the nature of your personal journey and understanding, and your ability to manage and keep the rest of your life in balance. I have always defined life in multiple quadrants. For example, my professional networking is completely different from the way I conduct my personal relationships around my church. The friendships in my self-development circle are driven by a totally different set of rules than when my wife and I work with young kids alongside my son. A careful nurturing of these quadrants – the spiritual quadrant, the mental quadrant, the physical quadrant and the social quadrant (which I will expand upon in the chapter on goal setting) – will help you determine how you can adopt a holistic approach to life, and cultivate a wide range of relationships. This is important, and I can vouch for it from my personal experience. The friends with whom I share a passion for physical fitness are so vastly different from those who have a more intellectual bent of mind. Each has a unique space in my life and I am that much richer for their contribution. Often, we do not have enough people in our lives who make a difference, because we live in a bubble of self-sufficiency.

Reference: An important step in establishing a circle of relationships or a network is a reference point with the individual you are trying to network. Discover a common idea, person or theme that can serve as a starting point for that person to begin connecting with you. I have found that even a simple remark about the weather will do, and it is amazing how folks open up and launch into conversation. Even assuming you never meet that person again, a casual conversation can sometimes be meaningful.

This happened to me as I made my way to Staten Island for the commencement of the biggest race of my life – the

New York Marathon – just when butterflies started flying at crazy speeds in my stomach. What if I could not finish? What if I were to go the way of the marathoner who died at the Chicago Marathon some years ago? What would my friends say if I fell apart at mile fourteen? Millions of thoughts were buzzing in my mind. But I also knew that the only way to overcome fear was to embrace it. So throughout my journey – in the ferry full of marathoners and on the bus ride to Verrazano Bridge, I kept talking to everyone who cared to listen and respond. And quite a few were happy to chat because it allayed all our fears. In addition to that, I got a few tips on how to stay focused. Some bits of advice reinforced what I already knew, which was great because it reassured me that I had the right inputs for my first marathon ever. A banker I met was running his eighteenth marathon, and another was running his twenty-seventh. Insane people, I thought to myself, and jokingly told another runner, 'It's like I've just joined a crazy cult!' He smiled and said, 'Or a big crazy family...'

Relevance: Networking is a bit like a dance. While you are covering common reference points such as education, interests, passions and hobbies, you are also simultaneously ascertaining how to make yourself interesting and relevant to the other person. If all you are interested in is finding out about him and how useful he is likely to be, and you make no attempt to present yourself in an appealing light, then how will you arouse any interest and hook him/her? So continue the conversation while managing to find points of relevance. For instance, if you were ever interested in something in which the other person is an authority, state it intelligently, draw him out, and get him to talk about it.

Let me illustrate the efficacy of this with a real-life example. More than thirteen years ago, in the city of Hyderabad, a couple of American writers, Cec and Sue, who between them have written about 150 books, visited the YMCA to conduct a writers' workshop. I participated in this, and in keeping with the tradition of *gurudakshina* and also a desire to get to know them better, I invited them for dinner and to make it a tad more attractive, I promised them Mexican food. They had been in India for about ten days and were looking for some respite from the 'rich' Indian food that was being served every day. Either because I was relentless or because my bait of Mexican food worked, they agreed.

As we sat down for dinner, I found that I was not able to establish any reference point with Cec, while I fared better with Susan. After a few minutes, I was beginning to get worried because Cec was unusually quiet and confined himself to some cursory remarks. Halfway through dinner, when the conversation had grown more and more contrived, I happened to ask Cec about his mission in life. Why was a man like him with such brilliant credentials travelling around the world to help emerging writers polish their craft? That did it! The way Cec slowly came to life was unbelievable. He turned the query back to me and helped me answer the very question that I had asked him. That was not all. Cec also helped me discover the role of writing in my life and how, eventually, it would determine my career and destiny. A reference point was established when I told him that I too wanted to write but had no idea where to start.

Many years later when I played host to him in my home in New Jersey, as he thumbed through the pages of my first book, I *Will Survive*, he was overjoyed. Our common interest had made that shy, reserved man come alive and even today he continues to inspire me in more ways than one, for he helped me transform myself in the area of physical fitness as well. Cec, who is nearly seventy, is a disciplined long-distance runner. Initially, when I began to take baby steps in this sport, he said, 'Keep going, buddy – I'll come by to your funeral and be a pallbearer.' I don't know what inspires me more, his sense of humour or his awesome discipline. Someone does not have to be super successful or a celebrity to be a source of inspiration.

Reach: Once you have established reference points with someone, take the relationship to the next level. Nurture it so that it goes deeper in reach. Who is on your speed dial? Who is that individual whom you can call in a moment of crisis, knowing with certainty that you have complete access? Who is that person, who may be at the other end of the world but never out of reach? The hallmark of a true relationship is the ability to pick up the threads anytime. How often do you call your friends without an agenda? When do you share something with a friend, knowing there is nothing you want in return? The principle of giving and investing in a relationship is applicable in all spheres of your life if you wish to forge strong bonds. Whether it is on a professional or personal level, no one will be around for you in your moments of need, if you haven't already prewired those relationships and invested enough of yourself in them. True friendships can happen in even the most competitive settings because individuals, even high-profile performers, are often lonely and respond to genuine friendship.

One essential key for networking is to dig a well before you are thirsty. As brilliantly pictured in the movie, 'The Godfather', if you have not pre-wired a connection, it will not come alive at the moment of need. The greater the significance of the person, the greater the need to cultivate the relationship. And do extend favours first before you seek one. Keep your contacts warm by constantly refreshing with updates and keep it growing by seeding it with helpful gestures.

Networking Myths

Beyond a point in the corporate world, it is not what you know but who you know. In fact, other things being equal, the ones who rise to positions of influence and visibility are those with networking skills. No matter how deep your technical expertise might be, if you are not a good networker, your growth will be hampered.

Networking is for everyone, right from the social butterfly to the reticent fly on the wall. It takes immense stamina, a desire to cultivate new relationships and preserve existing ones. But it is essential, and with adequate thought and planning it is eminently possible for anyone to succeed at it. In fact, you must make a networking plan and measure your progress on a periodic basis.

Myth: *I am not in sales or marketing, so I don't need to network.*

Reality: Everyone with a heartbeat – whether a professional, student or homemaker – has to network to be successful in influencing others at a professional or personal level, and for building a sense of community. No man is an island, and unless you live under a rock, and your job is to study rocks, you certainly need a network. You should always consciously try to meet and work better with other people, regardless of whether or not you ascribe the name 'networking' to what you do. In the olden days networking used to be through family or the family business or community circles. Today, the process of building networks has evolved further and is being constantly fine-tuned.

Myth: *I am into social service. I just help the poor, so my line of work doesn't involve networking.*

Reality: Wrong! Because influencing others to join the cause or contribute to it in some way, and the related lobbying for funding has increasingly become the order of the day. With so many noble causes competing for attention from donors, governments, lawmakers and policy shapers, as a social worker you need to know the key forces that are impacting society broadly, so that you can harness them better. In fact, the stronger your network, the stronger your cause and its visibility. Only if you have the right set of connections will you be able to open the right doors that will raise support for you and advance your cause as well as encourage volunteers to join in the effort. For instance, media-related contacts can spread word of your cause in various circles and bring you massive exposure which, in turn, could translate into funding. Unless you belong to an order of monks or nuns that requires you to take an oath of silence, it is imperative that you communicate, that you connect with others.

Myth: I *should be a gregarious, back-slapping party animal to be an excellent networker.*

Reality: That is partly true, and it helps if you are an easy conversationalist, adept at socialising, because those skills are needed at the ice-breaking stage of any relationship. But that is only the beginning. True networkers require as much discipline as construction site workers who stick to a plan and build exactly to specifications, one brick at a time. Few people have that natural flair for walking into a room and shining a spotlight on themselves with a grand entry, a smooth progression and a brilliant finale. Only the extremely powerful, or the rich and the famous can carry it off. All others have to create a plan and stay true to it, by meeting people, and cultivating friendships.

Myth: *Crowds overwhelm me; therefore I can never be a good networker.*

Reality: Like most myths, there is a part of that statement which is true. When you attend an event, or a large gathering, you might find yourself overwhelmed by the size of the crowd. But you can always eat an elephant, one bite at a time. True networkers realise that even if they meet ten people there, those ten ought to be so impressed that when you make a follow-up contact it immediately rings a bell, for the right reasons. This is best accomplished by meeting one person at a time, and treating him or her as the only person in the room, even if the place is teeming with hundreds of people. The impression you make by giving the other person such importance lasts a long time. Also, remember this cardinal rule when you present yourself to someone: you will never get a second chance to make a first impression.

Myth: I *have collected a bunch of business cards, so I now have a good set of contacts.*

Reality: Hundreds of business cards are thrust into the hands of those in positions of power. So it is your follow-up action that determines how the relationship develops and how strong it is likely to be, and not so much the first contact, which may have gone swimmingly well. True relationships, are built over a period of time with repeated touch points. In fact, the more powerful an executive, the more business cards he is likely to get, so it is important that you circle back faster than the others and get there first.

Myth: I *am already successful, so there is no need for me to network.*

Reality: Unless you are the President or head of a large nation, you need to network. In fact, the more powerful you are, the more the need to build consensus among the top league of players. If you are the big boss in an already successful company, unless you are retiring and handing over the organisation to someone else, you need to network as well. How can you future-proof your company's success if you cannot support its growth by continuing to build goodwill for the company? 'Make money and create goodwill' is the job description of most top executives. With an increasing number of hungry competitors, the need for greater support for the company is felt now, more than ever before. Not only do companies need to be successful, but their executives also have to get closer to government officials, activists, media-persons, and a wide range of differently wired stakeholders.

So networking is here to stay, and given the scale of the competition you are faced with today, you also need to be exceptionally effective at it, to make an impression and get things going your way.

To sum up

A 'caveman' has a narrow view of relationships, and this causes him to live in bondage, whether self-imposed or inflicted on him by others. On the other hand, an enlightened view of relationships wherein, like the marathon runner, you see others not as back-stabbing competitors, but as fellow cheerleaders, not only enriches your life but leads to genuine collaboration and relationships. You can never accomplish anything of lasting value single-handedly, so it is essential to hone your networking skills.

One of the defining moments in my early career days

was a chance encounter with a speaker who said "Love people and Use things" If you invert the equation, you end up loving things and using people, a sure fire mechanism to destroy yourself. The greatest tragedy is to spend your life scaling a mountain to find that there is no one around you to applaud. On the other hand, if you hike up a difficult trail on a mountain along with a bunch of like-minded individuals, the euphoria of accomplishing the task as a group far exceeds the joy of a lone ranger.

CHAPTER 4

From Leaders to Learners

How to Survive Challenges and Rise to the Top

Experience: that most brutal of teachers. But you learn. My God, do you learn.

– C. S. Lewis

In the earlier chapters, we explored the importance of cultivating a marathon mindset and discovering our calling for the purpose of breaking our 'chains' and escaping from our 'cave'. But after years of conditioning, our attempts to unshackle ourselves from our bonds and emerge into freedom could trigger problems and crises. So how can we surmount these challenges and emerge into the light? Once again, especially at the workplace, the answer is: rethink and re-evaluate what you have been doing all along, and get ready to make use of what you learn from this exercise, wherever you stand in the hierarchy of the organisation. To begin with, let's start at the top.

Go from Leader to Learner

There is an Americanism that aptly describes the situation in the corporate world: *too many Chiefs and too few Indians*. Everyone wants to be the head (that is, voice opinions and make sure things are done their way by everyone else), but no one wants to be the neck, or the shoulder or the hand. Moreover, the stereotype of a highly successful executive is the Machiavellian image of an aggressive, ruthlessly competitive, power-hungry individual, who is willing to step over everyone, spares no one, shows no mercy, and knows everything or atleast thinks he does. And such a leader invariably intimidates the people around him.

Fortunately, really successful leaders no longer conform to this pattern. In fact, there is already a work environment in India where bullying or high-handed behaviour makes people cry foul. Also, there is a growing school of thought that you can be cordial, compassionate and generous while climbing the ladder of success. Believe me, such an attitude actually works to your advantage. In the information economy, the old controlling, domineering styles of leadership that created pressure points in subordinates and peers have grown obsolete.

The information economy leader is cut from a different cloth. The information economy leader does not control or even aim to. He/she is willing to listen, change and adapt. Even so, the question remains. How does one lead without necessarily becoming all things to all people? Enter the Flexi-leader. Flexi-leaders are those who bend without breaking their core style of leadership. Increasingly, leadership has become all about effecting transformation, and enabling others to reach new levels of performance and new heights of achievement. All without burning out in the process.

A true leader is one who remains a learner all the time, and a learner disarms those he leads by constantly striving to learn and improve, and this, in turn, encourages others to follow his example and perform better.

So the other side of leadership is 'learnership'– everyone needs to learn, including the leader. (What's true for the leader of an organisation is true for the rest too for we are all 'leaders' in some area of our lives.) This chapter is about switching to the mind-set of a learner who repositions himself in changing times and milieus, so that his interaction with those around him is smooth and productive, and helps him overcome challenges and accomplish all that he wishes to, while enjoying the 'run'. Whatever your position, here are a few lessons that will stand you in good stead...

Nice Guys Do End Up Winning

You may be busy or frustrated at work, but that doesn't give you the licence to lacerate someone else. Unfortunately, corporate corridors are littered with the bodies of people whose careers have been sabotaged by those who did not care about others. If you try to achieve success at any cost, you'll be the only one celebrating in the end... but for how long? You would have made enough enemies along the way, who are waiting to pull you down. In the 'cordial versus cut-throat' debate, it is my belief that the former eventually wins. So stay cordial: it pays in the long run. If you are thoughtful of others and appreciate their work, pretty soon it will generate enormous emotional clout from which you will benefit. Your cordiality will certainly be reciprocated and other things being equal, you will get preference when you work with others.

During my advertising days, being cordial included buying snacks for the creative guys. Yes, it was bribery, but it was innocuous enough and it worked. Since I couldn't be a part of the smokers' gang or the alcohol gang, I had to invent a *mirchi-bhajia* gang so that I could get close to the creative fellows. The creative guys were known for their *dadagiri* and held us MBA types in much contempt. But for the sake of survival, I had to shed some of my inhibitions to bond with them. I had no help from a boss who was something of a bully, so I had to fend for myself, and I did it my way. Nice guys may finish last for a season, but in the long run it is the nice guys who end up winners.

'Win-some' or 'Loath-some', but Get the Job Done!

A winsome personality is the key to all-round success. No longer can functional expertise alone guarantee growth. Even if you are a technical person, sooner or later, you'll end up facing a client, or get on the phone with a customer. Also, it is only a matter of time before you start managing a group of colleagues for a project. So it is important that you acquire a portfolio of skills – including people skills – that will make you a well-rounded person, otherwise you will be forced to lead from your areas of competence (usually something technology based) and will find it difficult to rise and grow as you should. Excellent managers are those who can keep an eye on the scoreboard, while coaching their players to perform well. To be a coach, you need to be a savvy, people-oriented leader.

Learn to Press the Right Buttons

Genuine warmth opens more doors than you can imagine, and small gestures can take you far, so learn to press the right buttons. Of course, there will always be cynics who criticise every move you make, but then the cynical never get far, not with that attitude. You need to get the tough guys to let down their guard to break through to them and establish a genuine relationship. You cannot fake your feelings. Your concern must be sincere and come from the heart. And you must invest in these relationships without any expectations of professional benefits. Those are the by-products; the real end is to work together in harmony.

How to Navigate the Minefield of Office Politics

In today's scenario, there are very few areas that are not affected by politics, rivalries and bickering. People respond to this in various ways depending on their nature and attitude. If you are an Ostrich, you bury your head in your work and behave as if you are completely oblivious to your surroundings and the power dynamics unfolding around you. The Fox is a wily player and totally in the thick of the organisation's power play. The Owl, however, is aware of what is going on, but calmly focuses on work.

Usually there is a fight-or-flight response to most organisational politics. Either you get so involved that you become a vicious player or you try to distance yourself so completely from the goings-on that you are not aware of what is happening, and could end up an innocent victim. The savvy player is the one who diagnoses, discerns and deliberately decides to be an Owl; someone who finds a vantage point and wisely chooses to play only when it becomes absolutely essential. Owls are wise creatures. They can even take on bats, if it becomes a fight for survival.

A few months ago, I was told by a colleague – not exactly a pleasant one – that someone I work with very closely was frustrated with me. What shocked me was that this someone was very close to me and we often played tennis together, whenever we had time on weekends. I politely told this unpleasant colleague that I would only respond to email communication in such matters and had no patience with loose gossip where facts could be misrepresented.

Later, I called my tennis colleague and quietly explained to him that his careless remarks had given fodder to others who were trying to pull me down. While I readily accepted his apology, I also questioned his judgment in trusting everyone and babbling carelessly about a fellow worker. There will be times when you will be drawn into battles.

Make sure that you are calm and attack the issue, not the person, and handle things in such a way that it leads to an amicable conclusion. Otherwise you would have lost that person forever.

Most people either complain about the vicious nature of politics or just get so caught up in the killing fields that they lose sight of the nature and purpose of work. The right approach is to recognise that as long as people work together there are bound to be political alignments, and the smart professional goes through the maze unscathed causing little damage to those around. The key is to go beyond office battles and make a difference by mutually supporting one another.

The first step towards taking a benign view of the workplace is to believe that there are enough goodies for everyone... and that really is so! A marathoner believes that what is rightfully his will come at the right time, and unlike those who are caught up in politics, is not bent on devouring everyone around him. He is also mature enough to differentiate between what is worth fighting for and what is best left behind, even as you move forward.

Find Alliances and Meeting Points

It stands to reason that we will be happier and more productive if we look for common ground in our interactions with others, whether at home or at work, for that way we can build a rapport with them. But we humans have an incorrigible tendency to focus on the differences. Well then, how can we learn to zero in on the common factors?

Let's take an example from work. Say, you have a difficult colleague or boss, what are the ways in which you can find common elements that can forge a link? Over the past few years as an immigrant in the US, I have found that the best way to strike a rapport with someone is by asking some basic questions. There is an innate human need to talk about oneself, and I have found that by tapping into this and by showing an interest in others *without being inquisitive*, one can have sparkling conversations.

If the atmosphere within the organisation is dominated by mistrust, only the powerful leaders thrive and set the tone for the rest. When alignments are formed they are usually along the fault lines set by the most powerful leaders in the organisation. A smart professional does not take sides in an obvious manner, while fully remaining fully cognisant of the power structures. He builds alliances but wherever possible, he also finds common areas for collaboration and understanding, which give him enough leeway to forge strong bonds built on mutual respect and trust.

Show Genuine Interest in Others

So you think you have an open mind, but do you catch yourself stereotyping others? Are you able to overlook past experiences and give them a fresh chance? Are you forever going on about yourself instead of asking others to share their concerns with you, out of a genuine interest in them and not for the sake of gossip? If you've answered yes-no-yes to these three questions, you need to do something to revamp your attitude and show others that you are not as self-centred as you appear to be. So how do you show people you are interested in them?

First, jog your memory and link back past conversations to the current flow. Nothing surprises and impresses people more than when you remind them about their past conversations and, perhaps, refer appreciatively to one of their anecdotes or stories. I recently got back in touch with a professional trainer who had conducted a programme for us about twelve years ago. I admired him immensely, and as we conversed I enquired about his wife by name, in a very respectful manner. I was bonding without any 'benefit' expected, so you can well imagine his reaction.

In much the same way, over a period of time, I was able to work in politically charged environments and build genuine relationships. The first time I succeeded in this was during my early days in an advertising agency. There was a finance manager at the agency who was outspokenly critical of all of us in the client servicing department. He thought we were a bunch of suit-wearing upstarts who indulged in empty talk without doing any real work. While I was a client servicing manager, I had to regularly interact with this finance manager who spared no effort to make my life miserable. I found that almost no one wanted to have anything to do with him because he had an acerbic tongue and a loud voice that carried his jibes to the distant corners of the office.

Despite many earnest efforts to befriend him, I could not achieve a breakthrough... till the office picnic came around and all the families came together. I discovered then that he had two little boys, aged seven and nine, who like most boys were full of beans and mischief. I love kids and spent much of my time playing with the kids who had come to the picnic. So, by the end of the day, without any conscious effort, I had become friendly with every one of them, including the finance manager's boys. Because I was so used to having kids around me, at church, at the YMCA and in my own neighbourhood, I had had no difficulty breaking the ice with the family.

After that, as if by magic, things began to look up at work as well. There were times when I would ask the finance manager about his kids, and suggest how he could keep them gainfully occupied during the holidays, and since some of my ideas resonated with the family, I was seen as a genuine friend of theirs.

From being a target of criticism, I was soon included in his inner circle to whom lunch was sent, now and then. In fact, towards the end of my time in the agency, the finance manager and I had become such good friends that he would guide me in financial matters. The very mouth that spouted bitter complaints eventually ended up speaking positively on my behalf and even defended me against the criticism of others. When you build a genuine relationship, you are more productive because you work better together.

The second time such a thing happened was when I was in another multinational firm. Because I was from a different city, for quite a while I was seen as an outsider. And since the office in which I was seated was also the seat of the powerful, I was seen as a rank outsider. The department was run like a cartel led by a mafia don, and it took me many months just to get acquainted with the people there who behaved as if they were a gift to our organisation. They never had lunch with anyone outside their team, or mingled with the others. They spoke the local language and anyone who didn't was clearly not part of their clique. They were curt, often rude, and suggested that we go and talk to their boss, the CEO, if anybody didn't like what they said. Since they were handling a powerful department, no one took them on or even dared to befriend them. They were considered unapproachable.

Since they were hunting in packs, I figured that the only way to break into their group was to isolate each member and customize my approach. There was one member of the team who was fond of jokes and circulated them to his close circle of friends; I persisted in forwarding some jokes to him for a while, with absolutely no response from him. Finally, he relented and added me to his email group. And every time, he sent me a joke, I made it a point to say something light-hearted back to him.

A second breakthrough followed with another prima donna in the group – a haughty lady in a position of power, who was known for her credentials as well as her fiery attitude. Most people preferred to avoid her, but she had a soft spot that was too inviting to resist. On her desk, she had placed her little daughter's picture and the child, like all kids, was irresistibly cute. So I made some small talk around the child and since I also had a son who was roughly the same age, we hit it off. As the weeks went by, we invariably ended up chatting about the children's exploits, and like all doting moms this lady could not help talking about her genius-in-the-making.

One of the other members of the team was a cricket aficionado who had the loudest and strongest convictions on every conceivable topic relevant to the Indian cricket team. When he discovered – and I ensured that he did – that I was a freelance sports writer who was constantly interviewing cricketers, he softened up and had some 'interesting' conversations with me. I even organised a couple of tickets to a one-day game to which he took his eight-year-old boy. Another professional was an avid business news buff, and he would invariably quiz me on the writing styles of various magazines and journalists.

The leader of the pack was another equally inscrutable fellow with a tough exterior. After many futile efforts, I discovered that he was painfully conscious of his accented English. That had proved to be a major handicap as he found that he couldn't communicate forcefully with his team or with other employees. I offered to coach him and as I shared my own experiences in learning the English language, my own embarrassment at the guffaws I had evoked, we bonded well. I found out about some resources that opened up a few avenues and came up with suggestions that made sense to him, and gently prodded him on the road to learning. What came out of our pursuit, I have no idea, but in a year or so, I had the entire group eating out of my hand. In the cafeteria, I was the only non-team member who could sit at their table for lunch, and

I was offered coffee whenever I went to their department for work.

Word of this spread and my own teammates and supervisors in the city from which I had moved began to use me as their point man to get their own work done with this team, as they felt I had a strong rapport with them. Free lunches and drinks were offered in return for the removal of roadblocks and persuasive lobbying with the team. The more urgent the work that needed to be done, the bigger the incentive that was offered to me. Sometimes, I took them, sometimes, I didn't. But the point is that I had quite literally gone 'where no man had gone before'.

Don't Mistake Visibility for Credibility

There are some people who unabashedly want to rub shoulders with powerful executives in the hope that some of the glory will be reflected on them. Unfortunately, that is not true. Real power comes from knowing your position and operating strongly within your domain. The relationships help but only to the degree you bring value. Pure visibility alone cannot guarantee results. *Chamchagiri* or henchmanship may work in some organisations, but sycophancy can get you only limited mileage and you'll be exposed, sooner or later. In the meantime, you may also have alienated a host of others just by sucking up to the powers-that-be and ignoring everyone else. Instead, make a genuine effort to build relationships across the organisation, and you will be building a legacy for the future, while living a richer present.

State Up-Front What You Can Bring to the Table

When you interact with others, just as you are interested in taking something from the table, state clearly what you can offer, for instance, when you talk to an organisation with which you are dealing. Ensure that you articulate the benefits they will derive and do this compellingly enough to catch their imagination. You will probably be asked to send an email to follow up, or call, but you will usually be given the name of someone from their organisation for further action. Now that you have a name and – if you are charming enough – a phone number you can use for further transactions in future, you've got a foot in the door. Now it is up to you to decide how quickly you want to move the action along. Most often, if a top executive has given you a lead to someone else, you may be on the right track... or you have just been 'red–herringed'.

Beware of Red Herrings

Red herrings are deliberate decoys set up to distract 'stalkers'. Like you, many have trodden the path... pounced on unsuspecting executives, and delivered their sales spiel. Unable to extricate themselves politely, cornered top executives may turn you over to a player assigned for dealing appropriately with such 'stalkers'. A genuine request for business is usually dealt with respectfully and fairly, but pure celebrity chasing may not be encouraged.

Unless you have a worthwhile proposal to offer, you'll be seen as a stalker. And that is likely to cause resentment, and defeat the purpose of your networking. You are much better off trying to meet the person at an event that he may be attending, and hope that in spite of the crowds around the person you will find an opportunity to say something that makes a favourable impression. One cardinal rule is to offer your business card and hope that the person responds by giving you his. If he doesn't offer it, don't ask. Either the person has run out of cards or there is something else on his mind. By asking for his card, you may actually embarrass him as he might be forced to say, 'I am sorry, I've run out of cards,' or some such thing. If you have done your research well, then you know his office contact details, so politely offer to get in touch with his office for a further follow-up.

Make the Best of Conferences

When your company chooses you to attend a conference they are usually paying big bucks either to sponsor the event, or for your nomination. One sure way of making a good impression, particularly if you are keen to advance your career, is to attend every session well-prepared and make a significant contribution during the question-and-answer session. Again, preparation is the key to your strategy here. For instance, if there is a panel discussion on a topic of relevance to you, research the topic inside and out, ahead of the conference. During the time when the moderator or the emcee throws the session open for questions, stand up, introduce yourself, remember to thank the speaker or the panel first, and ask a crisp, clear question that demonstrates your insights and expands the scope of the discussion. The audience usually appreciates questions that either contribute to the conversation or offer a contradictory view. But the key is to be respectful of the panellists and the speaker. Never undermine the credentials of a speaker or the organisation he/she represents even if you do not think very highly of them.

Humour – particularly self-deprecatory humour – can come in handy, at such moments. Particularly, if you want to be the first to ask a question. It breaks the awkward silence while people collect their thoughts and debate whether they should ask a question. Secondly, it reassures the speaker or the panellists that they did all right and soothes their nerves. Finally, if your question is a good one, it paves the way for you to straightaway exchange business cards after the session is over.

However, if you were beaten to the first question by someone else, you have the opportunity to either feed off the first questioner, or offer a contextual statement and then take the discussion forward by asking your question. If you can offer a commentary on the session by comparing or corroborating what you heard in the other sessions, it will also enrich the quality of your question. Research is the key and the manner in which you carry yourself can contribute to your success. But don't hog the microphone, and start off at length for what you lack in depth. Every conference usually has an eccentric participant who will actually launch into another speech before restless organisers derail his attempt. You don't want to be another speaker. Crisp, compelling questions or comments are appreciated by all parties, particularly the speakers.

There are times when someone will say something to pre-empt your question. In such a situation your option is reduced to reaching out to the speaker on the sidelines of the event. Wait attentively in the line of sight of the speaker, and sure enough you'll get a chance to shake hands and speak a quick sentence or two. Watch the body language of the speaker and pace your conversation accordingly. Usually top executives attend conferences such as these with another colleague or associate. You might want to make your acquaintance with that executive too. Who knows, that person may actually be in a better position to facilitate the entry you are looking for. But be genuine in your effort to befriend him as well. Don't make it obvious that you are treating him merely as a means to an end. Always try and be courteous and cheerful.

Another oft neglected group crucial for networking purposes are the conference organisers. Take a moment to compliment them on the effort they have put into making the event a success, for the larger the event the bigger the stress on the part of the organisers. You want to build a special rapport with event organisers and constantly offer your support either in the form of feedback or in any other ways that are appropriate.

No matter which field you are in, each industry has professional bodies that should be your hunting ground. If you are not fully plugged into the network, you'll be left behind by more hungry professionals who are willing to invest in a set of relationships that are beneficial to their career. After you become a member of such a body, the next step should be to gain deeper access in that organisation. You need to get acquainted with each member of the organisation, particularly those who manage the memberships. Often, their work goes unsung, and any efforts to acknowledge their contributions are bound to create goodwill for you. The next step is to find out the committees and focus groups where your target executives serve. Once you know their agendas and their meeting schedules, figure out a way of getting your organisation to contribute to the industry body.

Your success in the organisation is directly proportional to your ability to generate value for others. Almost all industry bodies function on individual and corporate contributions and when you commit significantly to investing your time, effort and talent in them, you'll go a long way in building yourself up. The contacts you make will come in handy as you keep moving forward in your job. Also, industry trends, the shifts that are occurring and may impact you are first heard in the corridors of your industry body, before they hit the media.

Boost Your Humour Quotient

Blessed are those who can laugh at themselves; they shall never cease to be amused. If you want to rise, you need to be light: remember, you will achieve much more with a smile than with a frown. Also, the corporate world is in dire need of people who can take themselves lightly, now and then.

When I started to learn swimming much later in life, I would ferociously pound away at the water thrashing my arms and legs, till someone told me that I had better take it easy if I wanted to float lightly on the water. He also added that it was unlikely a six-footer would sink and die in a pool barely five feet deep, so I should relax and allow myself to float without getting into a frenzy.

Ah, the unbearable lightness of being light! Whether it is competitive sport, or the cut-throat corporate jungle, you have a higher rate of success if you can make yourself amusing, 'amusable' and approachable.

Humour can also diffuse a tough, tense situation, and is a key weapon in a modern warrior's arsenal. If you can leverage this tool, humour has the potential to take you far, so never underestimate its power. Among these three – wishbone, backbone and humour bone – the last one is the most important. He, who laughs, not only lasts but lasts longer.

Humour helps you connect with the people around you at a deeper level. Some big parenting challenges can be attributed to a communication gap that no longer allows parents and their children to laugh together. If a boss and a subordinate cannot share a joke – and I am not talking about the fake show of laughter put on by those who want to suck up to the boss, but authentic exchanges of humour – then there is something seriously wrong with their relationship. I have had the privilege of working with many types of bosses but the ones that I always managed to work well with were the ones with a sense of humour.

Want to bond with your team? Try a dash of humour. Let's say, as a team you have a common enemy in another department but you also need to work with him to make sure your team goals are achieved. Whenever he acts so insufferable that the collective blood pressure of your own team shoots up, you could try defusing the situation by mimicking him. That way, you are reducing him to a caricature that allows you to poke fun at him. When you do that, it helps the whole team to vent their frustrations quite harmlessly. But be sure that your motives are clean and that you are not using humour as a shield to launch hurtful attacks.

Humour helps you tread softly. You want to use this tool particularly if you are a new entrant in an organisation or group. When you laugh, you cut through the tension that those around you feel because you are seen as a threat that will disturb the equilibrium. When you can either laugh at yourself or fool around a bit, then those around you tend to lower their guard, and you'll find that you are able to break the ice and take your interaction to a warmer level. Believe it or not, you may not be remembered for how profound or brilliant you are but if you manage to make people laugh or better still, learn through humour, then you will surely leave a lasting impression. Humour is the hallmark of a well-rounded personality. In fact, the more stressful your workplace, the more the need to laugh and make others laugh. Take a look at all the charismatic leaders in the world, and study their character traits or leadership skills, and you'll find that they invariably had the capacity to make people laugh.

Not everyone is born fizzing with humour and the ability

to wow everyone around them. Like all skills, humour too doesn't come naturally to most people. So we need to consciously acquire it. One of my bosses had this terrific reputation of being able to tell jokes at the drop of a hat. Even when there were no hats to drop, you could count on him to come up with some engaging conversation that sparkled with humour, whether he was with his lunch group or participating in a conference call. Apparently, he had collected hundreds of jokes over the years and had a system of cataloguing them by occasion. He had also fine-tuned the art of cleverly adapting and using them to make humorous speeches. So it is no surprise that he was constantly called upon to make speeches. Unless you want to end up as an eminently forgettable face in the crowd, develop your humour quotient – yes, you can do it however quiet and introverted you might be – and here are a few tips to start you off:

- Compile jokes around your industry and what you do for a living.
- Develop some standard lines to introduce yourself, your place of origin, and so on. Say something unexpected... poke fun at yourself gently and make others chuckle.
- Practise narrating jokes in front of your kids, or close friends. The more jokes you tell, the more proficient you become at this. Of course, some jokes might fall flat either because you did not gauge the audience properly or did not deliver them well enough. Pick yourself up and keep moving.

My standard response when someone asks me what I do for a living is, 'I don't know', or 'I wish I knew', or 'No one knows' or something equally light-hearted. That sends the signal that I am not a pompous windbag bursting with self-importance, that I take myself lightly, and this encourages the other person to relax and engage a little more with me.

Like everything else, there's a time and place for such an approach, and of course, it has its limitations. To create a favourable impression, it is important to balance light-heartedness with commitment, and easy-going behaviour with a sense of responsibility. The ability to start with a certain amount of light-heartedness and quickly cut to the chase of formal business requires élan and maturity. We need to continuously evaluate the quality of our conversations to ensure that we get what we want while helping others get what they want.

Paint the Big Picture

Whenever you are guilty of any sins of omission or commission, it helps to paint the big picture. If there has been a similar situation in the past, recall it and refresh the group's collective memory. Salvage the situation by focusing on how to make everyone including your own organisation look good, and resist your fight-or-flight impulses.

Once you set an effective damage control mechanism in place, you can afford to lose the small battles while you concentrate on winning the decisive wars. Be available for clarifications, share your assumptions with others, and as long as your convictions are strong and the problems you may have caused weren't deliberate, you will be up and running again, although of course, you may not be able to win them all.

Take Responsibility for Your Mistakes

When you are responsible for a particular problem, assure those who are affected that you will resolve the problem as quickly as possible. If you continuously repeat and restate the crisis and the steps being taken to combat it, you will no longer be the centre of attention; you would have diverted the group's attention to the problem. Taking responsibility for your failures and shortcomings also diffuses the tensions between the teams. What can anyone say if you admit that a problem has been caused and offer to resolve it?

Knowing full well that mistakes can happen any time, remember to be sharply focused on your behaviour at work and carefully consider the choices you make. A casual approach invariably brings disaster to your doorstep. And what you are sweating about today, this week, this month will be exactly the same thing that makes you sweat a few weeks, months and years from now. So is it worth going on like this forever? There must be a better choice, a better way to work... right? But things will change for you only when you decide to change them, and flip the switch in your heart, mind and soul.

Beat Heat with Warmth

The key to beating the heat generated in a competitive environment is personal warmth. In the corporate world, and even in the world at large, there are two kinds of people: those who use heat as a weapon; and those who use warmth. The former group uses anger, aggression, rage, ambition, and power to beat you into submission. Either you cooperate with them or get burnt by their fury. You'll find them in every walk of life – bosses, colleagues and even members of the family sometimes try to dominate you with their forceful personality. You have to do as they say, or else...!

You either try to avoid such people altogether or give in to them. Both these options could leave you feeling dissatisfied or resentful. However, there is no need to be a pushover or plunge into unwanted battles. Take a deep breath, stand your ground, and deal with them quietly and firmly. In my work, I regularly meet such people. Often, I stop them in their tracks with some well-thought-out questions. Another thing that works is to ask them to explain their paradigms. But to take on such bullies at their own game, you need to be incredibly self-confident.

I was once part of an inter-department team that was being led by a bully. He was pushing through a set of guidelines that would have impacted my work adversely. Had I kept quiet I would have loathed myself for not speaking up and expressing my viewpoint. On the other hand, the group head was known for his abrasive tactics. In the end, I raised my hand and expressed my dissent. Backed by cold logic and without any show of emotion, I stood my ground and gave anecdotal examples and factual data that I was able to extract instantly from my laptop. I reminded the group head that we shared a relationship that went a long way back and that any difference of opinion on my part was by no means to be construed as defiance.

When confronted with the narrowness of his argument, he had no choice but to back down. He even asked for the opinions of the rest of the group. And when it turned out that they supported indirectly the line of argument that I had so doggedly pursued, he agreed, somewhat reluctantly, to incorporate my suggestions.

During the break, I found it awkward to approach the man whom I had deflated for my team's cause, but as we shared coffee, we laughed about some other 'idiots' who had pushed the group leader to the brink with their preposterous ideas! Being courageous doesn't mean you always have to roar or yell. If you care about something badly, there will be times when you are tested. Do make the distinction between the issue and the person. Otherwise, you will end up winning the argument and losing the person. And it is no secret that your bosses can either make you or break you. If you want to have a happy career, find out the areas where you can agree with your boss and put your entire weight behind him and his goals. You'll earn valuable currency that you can spend during the times when you cannot agree with him.

Insubordination in any form, active or passive, can harm your career. Once differences crop up between you and your boss or your organisation, it won't be long before you feel burnt-out. If you don't agree with something, state the reasons, and once the decision is made, fall in line and go the extra mile to do your job. Never give your boss the opportunity to pull you up for falling short. Only by enthusiastically putting your best foot forward, regardless of the circumstances, will you weather the storm... and subsequently, things could change for the better.

In the battle between heat and warmth, warmth always wins. Heat usually ends up burning people and leaving debris in its path. In the early stages of our career we usually focus on what we can achieve, but in a few years we begin to realise that achievements at the expense of people will certainly stunt long-term growth. So aim for a track record of achievements as well as genuine, long-term relationships. If you focus only on relationships, it will leave you with a large network of people but without any work-related trophies. And if you concentrate only on your achievements, you will end up with an admirable resume but without cheerleaders to celebrate your work. To get the balance right, you need to discover the difference between heat and warmth.

Empires and Emperors

You need to rise in the hierarchy if you are in an organisation, but it is only the naïve who believe that they can succeed in life purely by merit. Even if you are self-employed, you need to navigate through the customers' organisations to sell your wares. So either way, you need to sharpen your ability to understand people and power dynamics. In fact, the moment you walk into an organisation, you need to start adroitly making your way around, literally and metaphorically. Everyone who is in the organisation has the power to either help you or push you back, right from the front office executive to the head honcho. In fact, if you are in sales or have a job that involves relating with external groups, there are various types of power structures you need to map, and then position yourself suitably to get the job done. So never ever underestimate the power of the 'gatekeepers'.

A cardinal mistake most people commit while networking is to size up a person by the designation and schmooze with him accordingly. Power in an organisation does not depend on the designation of a person. It is usually acquired by strength of performance, depth of character, people skills and length of contribution. If you want to grow and get ahead, you network with only the powerful executives. However, if you want to create a lasting impact on an organisation, network with everyone, including the not-so-high-and-mighty ones.

Such networking savvy is crucial for survival not only in a corporate environment but even in bureaucratic circles. Often under-rated, the most powerful people who can either make things happen for you or block them forever are employees who are unseen in the decision-making chain, but crucial to it. Often, because you are in a hurry, you might confine yourself to tapping the top bureaucrats but neglect the officers who actually move the files. Anyone who has dealt with a government office can vouch for the frustrating snail's pace with which stuff moves in the corridors of power. Corruption often is not the only reason why stuff does not move. Government employees are also looking for recognition and for the human element in their dealings with people. In short, they want to feel that their contribution is significant.

During my sales career, I noticed that almost every effort I made to acknowledge such an individual and strike a rapport produced a positive response, and my friendly overtures were reciprocated. Not every sale that I made had to be achieved through a bribe. As they sensed a genuine effort to build a relationship, they loosened up. Yes, your work eventually gets done but patient relationship building paves the way for a smoother, quicker outcome.

'Map' Your Way to Success

It helps to 'map' people when you are trying to build relationships, and you need a wide array of tools for this. A friend of mine, a top-notch sales professional, actually prepares an organisational hierarchy slide of the key executives that he plans to contact for business. (Much of the information he is looking for is easy to access, as it is available on their website.) Then he systematically researches the key executives – their education, previous employment and designations. Since he has spent a fair amount of time in the industry, he usually finds a common contact or friend who can either provide an introduction or some insight about the person my friend wishes to approach. He even meticulously writes out and memorises what he needs to say when the time comes, for his motto is: *preparation, preparation and preparation*. Assuming that there are scores of others who are trying to cultivate this executive, who do you think will have the best chance of making an impact on him? Is it any wonder that my friend is on the fast track to success in one of the best corporations in the world?

Get Your 'Elevator Pitch' Right

Soon after you are introduced to someone, what you say in the first few seconds during the course of your opening conversation – your 'elevator pitch' – should make a permanent impression on the person you are trying to reach. This is what happened during my first meeting with Dr Ravi Zacharias, my long-time mentor and role model. In less than thirty seconds I told him, literally in an elevator where we were surrounded by others, how he had inspired me to be a communicator, through his sermons. By the time we got out of the elevator, I started introducing my friends to him. I am sure he met thousands of kids that year, but the earnestness and sincerity with which I reached out made a difference. However, what clinched it for me was that I established a common link by telling him that I had won a competition, which he himself had won many years earlier in Hyderabad.

Find such touch points, if you wish to build great relationships. And then, make the effort to keep in touch regularly, as persistence and timing are crucial for maintaining relationships. If you give the impression of being overly impatient, you are perceived as a pushy player, and if you are too laid-back, you miss the bus. You need to be perceptive enough to ensure that just the right impact is made, and at the same time that you don't overwhelm the person with unwanted attention. On the other hand, a good beginning could fizzle out because of a lackadaisical follow-up.

Build Bridges, Don't Burn Them!

Before I wrap up this chapter, let me touch upon something, or rather someone, who plays a vital role in all our working lives and is often responsible for everything from heartburn to thoughts of homicide in otherwise normal, peace-loving citizens – the BOSS! Of course, there are many, many marvellous bosses who are an inspiration to the entire organisation, but here's the buzz about the other sort of bosses – toxic, testy and terrifying – and the steps you can take not just to survive them but to befriend them as well!

Understand the Boss

I have a track record of working for every type of boss that one can come across in the business world. Right from arrogant bullies to generous mentors, I have interacted with the whole spectrum. Arrogant bullies who want to rule their empire with an iron fist usually create a culture of yes-men (although they are loathed by their subordinates). The bully boss is always the stud! Forget this at your own peril. A student can never eclipse the master, and he can rise only as far as the boss willingly raises him. Such a boss is a control freak, who views even the mildest form of dissent as insubordination and won't hesitate to embarrass, if not punish those who dare to disagree with him. So how do you tackle such a boss when you are taken to task for no fault of yours?

Sometimes, it is important to bell the cat in front of everyone. Once, during an inter-departmental meeting, there was a senior colleague who went hammer and tongs at me and my team. Everyone in the room knew that the criticism was directed at me and if I did not stand up for my team, I felt I would be doing an injustice to my calling. I picked up the threads of the debate and calmly stated my perspective. In fact, so outraged was I that I quickly accessed a few websites on my laptop and offered evidence to support my point of view. I conceded that there were nuggets of truth in what he was saying (I was confident I could convert this statement into a 'bridge' once tempers cooled although I had no illusions that it would be easy), but I emphatically countered his arguments and nailed the debate. Checkmate, as far as the verbal volleys were concerned. Yes, relationships matter, but your convictions and your calling matter equally, if not more.

Bully bosses pay only lip-service to the word 'team'. In reality, there is no team, except the one picked arbitrarily by him. The leaders that get the plum assignments are the unabashed bootlickers of the boss. And those who refuse to toe the line are usually branded and boxed in by the bully boss. Here, I must add that submission is not the same as subservience, but very few can differentiate between the two. Submission to a boss or an organisation is a volitional choice. Subservience is a helpless surrender to powers larger than you. Being a yes-man or yes-woman is subservience, but many are forced into this position, because disagreeing with the boss, however respectfully, invites retaliation that is swift and vicious. So they choose to surrender unconditionally.

Dictatorial bosses love such self-effacing individuals. They relish the unbridled control they have over them and manipulate them according to their whims and fancies. However, autocratic bosses and a bunch of helpless, hapless robots will not do the organisation any good. Secure bosses encourage autonomy. They prefer that their subordinates speak their mind, and let their feelings be known on every contentious topic before the final decision is made. Good bosses create the space and freedom for people to express themselves in a creative manner.

What bully bosses don't realise is that the organisation has placed in their hands immense power with which they can destroy or build, and such unbridled power occasionally corrupts. Unfortunately, such people believe that they have risen in the organisation by sheer brilliance and merit, and aspire to be better than their former mentors. What they do not realise is that they are behaving not like mentors but tormentors.

Often the line is crossed when the boss starts playing God with the lives of those who work for him. Because we don't have enough checks and balances in the corporate world, many an inept boss gets away simply by the power vested in him or her by the corporation. So are there any strategies to deal with difficult bosses? Or are you condemned to live with them and assume it is your karma to suffer? Over the years I have gathered the following insights and have learnt to work well with such bosses.

Understand Your Boss's Core Personality

Is it a conflict of working styles or personalities? This is the question you need to ask when two worlds – your boss's and yours – collide. Where is the conflict? Are you not satisfying your boss's expectations? Or is it about two different temperaments not being in sync? If it is a personality clash, there is precious little that you can do, except become more aware of your personality and consciously modify your responses. However, if it is about unfulfilled expectations, there is a lot you can do. First off, gather as much information about his or her management style as you can. As you keep talking and observing, you'll start painting a portrait of his preferences, pet peeves, work orientation, people management style, et al… And when you have a detailed and accurate portrait, you gain a closer insight into the person. If, for example, he is a martinet when it comes to time management and his meetings are run with Hitlerian efficiency, the last thing you ought to do is go late for one of them. If he has an insatiable appetite for details and seeks a report from you, you had better ensure that your report does not present just the big picture but goes deep into the nitty-gritties. Understand his core personality – otherwise you are setting yourself up for failure.

Understand Your Boss's Governing Values

Does he have a success-at-any-cost mindset, or is he a person with a clear set of principles, which govern his actions? How does he view his own boss? How does he view his peers? How does he behave in a social setting and in a one-on-one interaction? Is he on the fast track, or is he patiently constructing his own path to success? What are the items that adorn his office? Motivational posters? Trophies? Pictures of near and dear ones? Certificates and mementoes? These are some pointers that will give you a sense of what drives him as a person. Unless you have a thorough understanding of his values, you'll always end up playing a guessing game and be uncertain of the outcome when dealing with him.

In the final analysis, there are only two places where you stand in relation to your boss – either with him or against him. Simplistic as it may sound, you may lose out on many a promotion or reward simply because your boss didn't bat for you. So in the spectrum that starts from indifference and goes to the other end of intimacy, you'll have to figure where you are and, accordingly, come up with a plan to work with the boss. Remember, more than the competence that you bring to work each day, your orientation towards your boss can determine how happy and successful or otherwise you are at work, year after year.

In my world view, the best way to get ahead in your career is to make sure your boss is successful because of you. At least ensure that you've done your best not to impede his career goals. If he sees a threat in you, either because you are overambitious or you are getting too big for your boots, he'll ensure that you are cut to size. He might feel threatened because he not only has to manage competition from his peers, but will now have to manage a super-talented, potential competitor in you as well. Those who try to get ahead of their bosses will surely be pushed back, at least to begin with.

Employees in most corporations tend to make an exaggerated assessment of their contribution and work, and speak disparagingly of others, notably those who are senior to them. 'He is such an idiot... how did he get there in the first place?' is a commonly expressed sentiment. While there may be nepotism at work, more often than not, someone got there because he or she did something right, or someone thought they could do something right. Either way, some humility can alleviate a lot of pain and suffering at work. Each time, you are denied a promotion you can sulk, throw a tantrum, or take it in your stride and quietly ask yourself if there is something you could have done differently. When I ask myself that question, amazingly the answer I usually get from within is that I made a few errors myself and paid the price for it.

I am not discounting the bosses who ride on the shoulders of their subordinates. The corporate world is full of bosses who think, 'Ask not what I can do for you, and instead ask what you can do for me'. If you are stuck with such a boss, your best option would be to support him while you can and quickly move before the resentment and frustration set in. If your contribution was genuine and verifiable, you'll have no problem creating momentum for yourself and get a lateral entry to another organisation in the same industry.

You Can't Keep a Good Man Down

I once had a vicious supervisor who would walk all over his own mother to get somewhere. Whenever we achieved something, he would say, 'We did it as a team.' But when the increments and awards were announced only he would get the accolades. This caused a lot of heartburn in the entire office. Our organisation was sinking at the time, and in fact what kept the branch bobbing above the waters were two of my key projects. Nothing worked with him, not one-on-one confrontations or group representations. He was just plain insensitive to others. Relentless in his pursuit of personal success, he progressed rapidly. In fact, too rapidly, for he was promoted... Sure, he made his money and enjoyed the rewards while they lasted but he was exposed for what he was and sacked shortly after his promotion. If only, he had taken his people along with him on the road to success, it would have been a different story.

Contrast that with the type of leader who is willing to stand by his people no matter what. He stands shoulder to shoulder with his team during moments of crisis and is such an inspiration to others that he has almost a cult following. Such a leader has a genuine, palpable connection with his team, and clearly sets out what he can do for his people and what is expected from them. Such a boss commands respect not because of his designation but because of his personality and character. Much as he needs to toe the management line for reaching corporate goals and objectives, he is also in a position to influence his line managers to perform at their peak simply because of the loyalty he is able to command.

There is a saying in the corporate world that 'people don't change jobs, they change bosses'. Like most clichés, there is a ring of truth to it, and the future belongs to those who are willing to be vulnerable and lead people with genuine empathy and conviction.

The *Mai Baap* Culture

Bosses are larger than life in India, although the culture is changing in New Age industries like IT and biotech, and will eventually change in others as well. Even today, in some traditional industries, bosses don't mind being worshipped. Surely hero worship is appropriate if they are national icons or sports stars. Only a wimp worships a boss. Of course, there are role models who cross our path and we can and should draw inspiration from them. Every individual has the right to be treated with dignity and just because we work for a living does not mean we can be robbed of our self-respect and dignity. In earlier times when jobs were not plentiful, people would suffer silently at work. Women were subjected to harassment simply because they were vulnerable. Powerful bosses used their office to satisfy their personal needs and egos. Today, thankfully, with increased awareness such obnoxious characters are being taken to task.

The proliferation of opportunities has truly freed many of the oppressed from the fetters of these slave-drivers. There is a difference between stretching your people for excellence and pushing your people over to destruction. Often the line that demarcates the two is only visible to the mature manager.

Organisations that don't reward managers who manipulate their people tend to go for the long haul. Mere lip service to employees and their importance results only in empty chatter. When employees can truly sense that they are respected and their value is not just in numbers, they will rise to contributing beyond what is expected of them. There is a power that is unlocked when genuinely motivated employees hitch their dreams to the organisation's mission. Such a motivated army can move mountains, win gigantic battles and create history, not just for their organisation but shape the economic destiny of the country. I had the good fortune of meeting some of the finest business leaders in India during my career as a PR manager and as a freelance journalist. One of the main reasons for their success was their ability to draw an individual to commit his dreams to the organisation. Only when an individual is convinced that he is on a dream team working on a dream project, will he contribute his best. When managers grasp the reality that an individual is more than his work, they will be able to inspire their team.

Here is what I learnt from my cross-cultural experiences.

- Map every individual and seek to understand the person first.

- Screen your own baggage and world view and consciously explore common areas when you interact with others.
- Build relationships without any expectations. Work follows much later.
- Offer constructive feedback and comments that build people.
- Identify touch points and keep feeding them with interesting inputs.
- Give every individual the opportunity to brag about his or her strengths, likes, pet peeves, in short, anything at all, in order to build a rapport with them…

To sum up

Every organisation poses a unique set of challenges. Adaptability is the key not only for survival but also for serving in a meaningful manner. Spend time connecting with people in a genuine, open manner and show that you care. Your ability to invoke trust and inspire confidence is the precursor to success. After a while, your reputation will precede your work.

CHAPTER 5

From Slavery to Service

It is better to shun the bait, than to struggle in the snare.

- Ravi Zacharias

Generally speaking, there are two kinds of employees: those who believe that there are enough goodies to go around and that each and every one will get a fair share; and others who are forever struggling with nightmares of scarcity, and try to grab as much as they can before the gravy train passes by. It is crucial to recognise this because your outlook shapes your behaviour and the choices you make at work, as well as your contribution to the organisation and how you fit in there.

What if you feel like a misfit and in spite of all the pains you have taken to do things right, your life seems to be spiralling out of control? How can you pull yourself together and recharge your energies, deal with the power equations and weather the storms at the office, if the root cause of your problems are your boss, colleagues or subordinates? If you find yourself in the hot seat (maybe, because you are not in sync with the work culture of your organisation), how can you learn to fit in without forsaking your principles and straying into a path that you are not comfortable negotiating because it means compromising your values? What if you are frustrated because of where you are in relation to the others around you? Well then, maybe, the time has come for you to take a good hard look at yourself and make some changes.

Redefine the Unit for Measuring Success

If you are measuring success by what the majority of people in the business world do, then you are setting yourself up for disappointment. There will always be someone who will outrun you, out-earn you, and out-perform you. The corporate environment is a cauldron of simmering discontent. If you can look within and set your own standards, and are no longer dazzled by external allurements, you will be more at peace when things do not go your way. I have found that no matter how I fare in my performance appraisal each year, knowing that I have run the race well gives me a tremendous rush. No matter what your company thinks of you, what the man in the mirror thinks, counts. And counts a great deal!

In most corporations, the few weeks after the annual increments are announced are turbulent days. There is a lot of heartburn among those who thought they would get the pot of gold at the end of the rainbow but came up empty. Then there are the opportunistic players who wait for a raise, so that they can use it as a baseline to negotiate a better salary with the next employer. If you are measuring your career progression only in terms of money or high-speed growth, then you'll soon hit a burn-out phase and disillusionment will set in. Rewards and financial gain ought to be side benefits while you pursue your life's mission. But if your mission is just to translate your work into monetary units, then you have a narrow perspective of things, which will leave you dissatisfied in the long run. Broaden your vision, come up with worthwhile goals and chalk out a long-term plan to accomplish them. And yes, it will take a reasonable amount of time – after all, it is not a cup of instant coffee that you are making here.

Go, Dig a Well!

Go dig a well before you are thirsty. Plan in advance to harness the resources you will need for your life's journey. The social well is your network, the spiritual well is your relationship with God and your physical well is your reservoir of wellness and health. If you do not make an accurate assessment of your resource wells and monitor them regularly, you might find that you're left high and dry during a crucial part of your journey. So are there moments when you find that your wells seem to run dry? Times when your relationships flounder and you feel desperately vulnerable... times when life seems so hopeless that you want to cover yourself with a huge blanket and disappear forever... The term 'rock bottom' is used to describe moments like these when you run out of answers, and find yourself stuck in a problem that seems to have no solution, and everything you touch seems to turn to ash. No wonder someone once said that ulcers are not caused by what you eat but what eats you. Stress ranks among the top killers in any society and one doesn't have to go further than the daily newspaper to discover what havoc heightened stress levels at work have caused, in this country.

Life-changing events such as death, divorce, financial loss or failure in examinations could drive us to desperation. Our ability to cope and our well-being depend on how deep our well is, and how often it refreshes itself. The beauty of any well is that it has the capacity to refill itself. As long as we are constantly drawing from the well, and tending to our needs consciously, these wells serve like deep cisterns, refreshing and refuelling us as we go our way. Which is why, the scriptures exhort us to pay attention to our heart, for it is the wellspring of life.

You Are What You Are, Not What You Do

People who brave adversity and survive the vicissitudes of life without crumbling invariably have three qualities: resilience, strength of character and depth of personality. It does not matter how many times you fall, what matters is how many times you get up. So even when you have been knocked down, how do you make sure that you are not knocked out? How do you develop the ability to bounce back to life?

Begin by making a conscious effort to view success and failure as temporal, and separate them from yourself as a person. If you can understand and accept the fact that just because you have failed at something does not make you a failure, then you have an excellent starting point. Conversely, just because you have succeeded at something doesn't make you a success. Separate your failures and achievements from your core personality. You are not what you do, you are what you are. Your character is distinct from your resume. No one ever puts down their failures in their resume. However, you can always turn your learning experiences into insights that you can use for painting your life in a different colour.

Be True to Your Principles

After separating your personality from your calling and career, the next step ought to be to define your orientation towards success. How far will you go in pursuit of your goal? If you know that you are twisting or stretching your truth to achieve a certain goal, will you pull back or proceed anyway and savour your success? In other words, what are the values that define your success? In my pursuit, I have always found that there are certain things I would not do even if I were paid a fortune. For instance, I will never work for a company that makes alcohol or for a tobacco company simply because my values are in direct conflict with what I would have to peddle in my quest to make a living. I have long discovered that there are some folks who can rationalise anything as long as it suits their convenience. But there is a tremendous sense of liberation when you stay firm and declare to the world that you stand for something. And that if what you stand for conflicts with what's on offer, regardless of how attractive it might be, you cannot be bought.

A few years ago, I was contemplating two job offers and like many situations in life, both were equally appealing. How on earth was I to decide? I knew full well that once I chose a certain offer, the other would be closed to me for a long time. So I asked myself, which of the two companies would be more in sync with my values. I decided to dip into the collective wisdom of my friends to get a fuller picture of my options. As it happened, the clincher was the discouraging feedback I got about the company I was leaning towards and, after some thought, I ended up rejecting their offer. (Someone once said: 'Whenever you are stuck between two hard choices, toss a coin. You may not get the right answer but while the coin is spinning in the air, you'll know where your heart is.')

'No matter where you work,' I told myself, 'since that's where you are going to spend the bulk of your waking time, it is important that you feel comfortable in that environment.' Consonance with my values and world view was the clincher for me, and fortunately, it worked out well. As the saying goes, 'In matters of principle stand like a rock, in matters of fashion, be flexible' if you wish to sleep well at night.

Think Before You Charge into Battle

There are bound to be pinpricks in any corporate environment (and elsewhere as well), regardless of how carefully you choose your job. So have a perspective of time when dealing with office politics. Think calmly and ask yourself, 'Will this matter in a few days from now, in a few months, in a few years?' Suzy Welch, wife of management leader Jack Welch says that she applies the 10-10-10 rule before making any decision. Will her choice matter in ten days, ten months and in ten years? If the answer is no, then it is not worth the battle.

Knowing which battles to pick will help you go through life with fewer hassles. However, there are some who are always raring to pick up every gauntlet that is thrown down anywhere in the vicinity, in their zeal to annihilate anyone who crosses their path. Sure you'll meet dogmatic, opinionated, inflexible and often, stupid individuals, powerful enough to rock your world. But then what did you expect? A happy, clappy world that would roll out a red carpet for you all the time? And there will be times when you will be outsmarted and beaten, maybe, even humiliated by others. Ask yourself this question, 'Do these guys matter?' You can either fight them and keep collecting heads as trophies, like ancient tribesmen, provided you manage to defeat them. Or, if you know where you come from and where you are headed, you could brush aside these irritants, take a larger view of your own journey, and decide to let go. Tread softly; you have far more important battles to fight, so rise above the corporate politics and games of narrow-minded individuals with petty egos.

The larger perspective might even allow you to look upon such players with sympathy and compassion. Perhaps you can destroy them in one fell swoop, but is it worth the politicking? Once you get to that level, you'll set off an unending volley of punches and pretty soon, the original issue will get blurred as personality attacks take over. Nip battles in the bud before they grow like weeds and consume everyone. Graciously bow out. Meekness is not weakness. It is the courage to rise to a higher ground. Dexterously move the debate beyond personality, and reframe the dialogue keeping in mind what is best for the organisation. If you are not happy with what is being demanded of you, offer another alternative, and demonstrate your willingness to serve and produce the required results, although not necessarily on their terms.

Shore Up Your Self-Image

Your self-image cannot be so easily shattered that one forceful personality or bully can trample all over you... unless *you* allow it. The dictionary defines the word 'individual' as 'something that cannot be divided, a unit'. And your personality – the sum total of your being – ought to be so strong that when you are buffeted by upheavals and crises, your mettle may be hammered but you are never broken.

Over the past few years I have been a student of human behaviour and have discovered that individuals who refuse to let their self-respect be compromised are treated better. Your self-image determines how others treat you, as well as most social outcomes. So in your dealings, let people know that they can disagree with your ideas, but with due respect and without trying to ride roughshod over you.

Many years ago when I was planning to leave the country, a senior colleague advised me to consider moving to another department where he could personally mentor me. Flattering though it was it meant that I had to quit my core area of marketing and join another team. However, this senior colleague had a reputation for building a cult following. Either you belonged to that cult or you were an outsider. Again, I evaluated the situation carefully. I asked myself whether my way of working could gel with his attitude. Would he allow me the liberty of expressing a contradictory opinion or would I be reduced to a robot? Was it not likely that a team headed by him would end up like a bunch of assembly-line products conforming to his design? Finally, my self-image helped me make the decision to politely refuse the offer, even if it meant alienating him for a while. I felt the long-term implications were far too serious to ignore.

Often employees become helpless pawns when powerful bosses or team leaders with their own agendas determine the way forward. Consciously steer clear of any office politics, focus on your work, and give it your very best. After all, your work is in your control while office politics can sap your energy and time. I am not proposing that you bury yourself in work like an ostrich. Quite the contrary. The savvy employee knows the political equations in an organisation clearly. In fact, it is this very awareness that helps him rise beyond power equations and constantly strive to excel at his work.

The most instinctual response the moment you join any

organisation is to be seen as the boss' miniature. Resist the temptation. Make your own space. Create your own identity. Don't buy into all the legends and fables that you are told. Discover it yourself. Chances are that you'll find that once you begin your own search, those 'enemies' are not enemies but folks with genuine concerns and you will surely discover common ground. Perhaps you can make a difference. Don't let your shoulder be the placemat for your boss or someone else to train their guns. Or agendas. 'Surely, that would amount to insubordination,' you may say. 'Won't my boss hate me, if I voice my independence?' Not if you can demonstrate that by thinking for yourself you are opening up new options. Your boss may hate you for standing up for your own convictions, but if you can deliver value to your team, not only will you stand vindicated, but your self image will be reinforced because you did what was right for the organisation. Isn't that how everyone is supposed to work anyway?

The organisation and its vision and mandate are far more important than anyone's individual agenda. A savvy individual knows how to make a contribution through work while harvesting great relationships. Your character will determine whether you'll play petty games or focus on fulfilling your life's mission by aligning it with that of your employer. In fact, so strong ought to be your conviction that you should be able to inspire colleagues whenever you speak about the organisation. The moment you lose focus and turn your eyes towards yourself or the promotion or the rewards, then you are playing the game with a different motive.

Why is it that some people can go on relentlessly while others keep losing their steam at regular intervals? I think the answer may come from their motivation. The root word for 'emote' is the same which means to move something. Our spirit is galvanised and moved by the vision that we have for ourselves. When we are able to align our vision with something larger, then we are moved.

'It Is Well with My Soul'

When problems and sorrows come rolling by like sea waves, can you still say, 'It is well with my soul'? It is not without reason that this particular song became one of the Mahatma's favourites. Don't let the anxieties of tomorrow weigh you down. Fight the battle one day at a time, and give it your best. Then you will truly be an evangelist at work. In the corporate world, there is a real paucity of people who can take a longer-term view of the projects at hand, and at the same time guide teams, one milestone at a time, one transaction at a time.

If your vision and mission provide you with the compass, it is this ability to look at day-to-day transactions that will help you progress, one day at a time. When you walk in to work each day, it is this ability to flit between the transactions and tasks that drain your time and also view the big picture at the same time that will make you a great professional. If you must be 'corporatish', remember that it is the ability to strategise as well as implement. Often there is a dichotomy, but in my opinion those who are good at strategising are usually hands-on as well. But if you are stuck with operations or transactions all the time, you'll never graduate to running teams or departments because you are more a doer than a manager who can get things done through others.

How to Eat an Elephant

It happens sometimes... first, an overbearing boss, and then, an overwhelming mountain of work... so what can you do to survive? You could either go under, or explode and blow away everyone who comes your way, or take a deep breath and say, 'Welcome to just another day at work,' and smile! Outlandish, as the suggestion may seem, once you smile, your 'positive chemicals' start kicking in. Crack a joke, or switch gears, or completely switch yourself off from the task at hand, or walk around for a couple of minutes and ask yourself, 'What is the one thing that will ease my anxiety, if it is taken care of?' In other words, discover the big elephant and attack it first. And, in course of time, you will find that the elephant gets smaller and easier to eat, and you will soon have things under control. (It helps if you switch off your cell phone and stop opening emails!) So how does one eat an elephant? One bite at a time.

Now that you've taken care of the huge, big, intimidating elephant, start chasing the little ones. Return your calls, check your emails, and take a deep breath again to see if you are still operating on adrenaline or breathing normally. It is never a good idea to constantly rush from one heady, high pressure environment to another without pacing yourself and taking a breather. You don't have to be busy

24 x 7, or put on a show for people as I used to do, once upon a time. Even when I was rushing off to loaf with someone in another department, I made sure that I carried something suitably official looking in my hand to convey the impression of being busy!

Get Rid of the Mask

Some people put on a mask and pretend to be something else at work, or give the impression that they are doing things that they are not. Get rid of the mask, and instead build authentic relationships on a foundation of genuine integrity, for they will go with you wherever you go. Sure there is a professional decorum that calls for a different set of choices to be made at work. But your persona doesn't have to change fundamentally and there is no need to shun the human touch in professional or business interactions. In fact, the more genuine you are by peeling off your mask and letting your guard down, the better your chances of building a rapport with others, and working more effectively yourself.

To sum up

You are a unique individual. Do well to remember that. You are more than your work. But, so is everyone else on this planet. Have a strong, well-thought through set of beliefs. And stand up for them. And always, BE YOURSELF!

CHAPTER 6

From Hungry Plodder to Happy Worker

No man ever got very high by pulling other people down.
The intelligent merchant does not knock his competitors.
The sensible worker does not work those who work with him.
Don't knock your friends. Don't knock your enemies. Don't
knock yourself.

– Lord Tennyson

Reorienting your workplace-thinking

The hyper competitive world is built on a win-lose paradigm where many jostle for a few rewards. The only guarantee is the probability of a plethora of factors that are at play that determine whether you are an outright success or a downright loser. The best way to ensure success and enjoy the journey is by constantly rewriting the rules, not just for others but more for yourself. This reorienting yourself has two huge benefits. First of all, it removes the huge pressure from yourself to succeed at all costs. Secondly, it gives you the perspective to enjoy the moment, to smell the proverbial roses along the path.

When you realize that no matter how hungry the other person is to use you, you will still focus on yourself and not on others, you call the shots. You will never surrender the locus of control. Even at the risk of being vulnerable to being manipulated, you know that since you are almost in a state of nirvana, you take the higher position of fulfilling all your responsibilities to the best of your abilities and with a smile to boot. Not counting the immense good such a posture does to your overall health, it liberates you to focus on what's really important for you.

Your transactions become stepping stones for deeper relationships which enrich your spirit. When you add a series of transactions, you build a track record of collaboration and trust which places you on a much stronger promontory than the shifting sands of outmanoeuvring that forever threaten your equilibrium. When your trustworthiness grows, your network becomes a rich deposit of resources that not only keep adding but also can always draw from, should you ever need.

When you are not obsessed with the prize but are keen on giving of yourself, people respect you instinctively. That respect often translates into moral authority to confront others. Often, I find myself in situations when I have to do the uncomfortable job of calling out fouls. Whenever I do that, I always appeal to the transaction record of the individual in the past and ask them why they either broke my trust or did something to jeopardise my image. Because I am appealing from a strong high ground of evidence, they usually apologize. At that point grace kicks in and I realise the need to not beat them down further. I quickly move on to discussing business as usual. Since the other person has now acknowledged the error, there is no point in gloating over the wrong… No wonder the wise saying goes "Love covers a multitude of sins." Love may cover a multitude of sins, but Judgement confronts tenderly.

In recent times, I have had to handle awkward situations wherein I had to confront multiple colleagues on a project. Much as I enjoy working with these folks, I had to call a time out and speak my mind to ensure the success of the project. "You did not cover yourself in glory", I told them as I appealed to their usual standards of excellence and because I was not combative but firm, they were also not unduly resistant to my feedback. I am not always the type who would quickly roll over and die, but there is no need to strut around with authority or throw rank where it is not needed. The timeless principle of "Appeal to the individual's self-interest" always works. I felt good because I was able to quickly intervene without necessarily offending anyone in the process. While I am not making gender – based suggestions, the approach depends on whether you are talking to a male colleague or a female colleague because the tone and tenor differs based on the target audience. With my male colleagues, I usually take a carefree and a heart to heart approach and with my lady colleagues, I usually try to think through my exact approach and language in advance. However in any situation, a strong relationship is the foundation, even for unpleasant but necessary conversations.

From win/lose to win/win outcomes – Strive to win the person while winning the transaction.

One of the handy tools I picked up during my business school days was the Blake and Mouton grid which explains the interplay between tasks and relationships. In short, it defines all individuals as either high achievement oriented or high task oriented. A leader is defined as one with either a high concern for production or people, as it was conceived in the 1960s. In today's society, any colleague can be classified on that scale as someone who is driven either by Results or Relationships, the ideal scenario being a high obsession with both.

If there is a dominant paradigm that I cannot stress enough, it is that possibility that true results can be achieved through an obsession with people. If you love people, you use things. But if you use people as things, you end up losing in the long term. People ought not to be used for your progression but enriched along the way. Only myopic individuals play the dangerous game of using people to get ahead. I had to learn a lot of hard lessons along my life's journey to discover that bitter truth. While I have a wide range of aspirations, I was never truly ambitious. The thrill of enriching myself and others along the way was intoxicating enough. There will always be the overambitious colleague next to you, plotting and scheming to get ahead of you. There will always be the overzealous colleague who will openly flout rules to outplay you. Turn your focus inwards and ask yourself, if you ought to be sucked into their vortex, or if you want to play the game your way. If it is the latter, then you can win the person and not lose him or her. If you look at all the "unfair" stuff that happens around you, you'll pretty soon start feeling bitter or like a martyr and give in to despair. Such negative feelings drain you and reduce your work to drudgery. Not quite the happy situation you want to be in! On the other hand, declare your intent to play it your way. Write down a few rules that will never be broken and boundaries that will never be crossed. That posture takes you to a tremendous high from which confident, and competent work flows.

A corporate job does not offer you the luxury of retreat. You are constantly in a battle mode. Unless you are clearly aligned to your internal true north, you'll never be sure footed. It is alright to lose a short term battle to win a war. It is alright to make someone else look good, without necessarily making yourself equally good. It should be alright to let someone else gain glory as long as you are not being seen as the vanquished. There is a great degree of happiness in cheering others. Your ability to be seen as a generous enabler of other's success can actually be a platform your own good.

Here are a few pointers on how you can become a better collaborator.

Ask great questions

In every transaction, if you feel it is leading to a situation of win-lose, ask the question, how can we make this transaction good for both of us or our teams? Shouldn't the outcome of success be where both teams can find acceptable outcomes?

In fact, the very process of asking such questions opens up avenues that have not been hitherto explored. The other benefit of asking such questions is that it clarifies to each other their own tacit and explicit expectations. The corporate world is full of disillusioned and disappointed people who have become that way because their expectations have not been met. If we constantly ask great questions, then even those who are driven purely by assumptions are stopped dead in their tracks, to clarify, think through and state their expectations. A quick conversation is better than a hundred exchanges on an email trail. A short, face to face meeting accomplishes a lot more than email trails that last days and weeks. Email serves audit purposes but great accomplishments happen when expectations are clearly stated.

Explain positions early and clearly

Every transaction determines a winner. Some ruthlessly clean the table without leaving anything to the other party except resentment. Often it is not a good idea that a winner takes all. By definition, someone wins and the other party loses face, but it does not have to be that way, if we can rewrite outcomes in a manner where both parties can win.

Provided it is stated early on, that you are in it to win it, for both parties. What cuts through borders is when you act like you are trustworthy and commit to ensuring the best outcome for the other party. That gives them the permission and confidence to give themselves totally to the transaction. It is not rocket science, but often it is these basics of trust and dependence that are violated in the corporate world. Remind those who are straying from the promise gently that you are still committed to winning it for them, but you cannot do it single-handedly and they ought to work along with you.

Explore new alternatives by unchaining your views

Often either because of the sheer busyness of the day, or plain laziness, folks do not brainstorm enough to explore new alternatives to achieve goals. If you get into the trap of 'my way or no way', then you are limiting yourself as well as the organization's potential to achieve more. Ask if anything new can be done to accomplish the same goals. Go to multiple sources, think of new options and you will be richer for the times ahead. But if you treat a transaction listlessly, not only will the outcome be mediocre but you will have lost a great opportunity to build a new relationship and cover yourself in glory. This approach always allows you to have a plan B or in some cases, multiple back-ups. What if the coveted promotion does not come through, because of a jealous boss? What if you do not get the desired project but get hand me down stuff? What if you were on the fast track, but are asked to do something that will slow you down? A week or a month in the corporate world is never the same, but if you are well prepared, nothing can shake your poise and inner confidence because you are prepared with detailed alternatives.

One of the reasons I never place a lot of emphasis on my job is because I never let it define my identity. My identity ought to come from who I am as a person, not what I do for a vocation. During the early stages of my career, I attached a high importance to designations and titles, but in the current season of my life, I am discovering that those who lead without fancy titles are the true leaders. To a certain degree, these titles explain or describe an individual's skillset but the title is not the person. To mistake that the role is the individual is robbing the person of tremendous dignity and value. There is inherent merit and respect in every person, both in the corporate world, and outside. Any attempt to glorify individuals based on titles is to undermine others without those fancy designations. While I am in awe of individuals who have accomplished a lot in the corporate world, I never get overawed by their business cards, simply because the person is so much bigger than his work. Such an ethos underpins every enlightened person's interactions with others. If you do not value their dignity and their talents, then you are placing yourself on a higher pedestal and that does not lend itself to facile transactions.

Early on in my career, I developed a reputation of having contacts practically everywhere. Not because I envisaged a job in Public Relations, but because of my friendly nature. As a result, I used to be asked to help even by friends who had friends who needed a favour. Without expecting anything in return *(OK, maybe an occasional biriyani!)* I would marshal my network to get stuff done for others. Little did I know that someday, I would actually end up in a profession that entailed working with influencers. After 25 years, when I look back, my training for professional success commenced long before I had a job. The desire to help, the desire to influence others and a strong sense of reaching those in need actually pre-existed before the corporate world actually gained the benefit of my skills. When you take immense pleasure in helping others, you are actually raising yourself in the process because you cannot but help yourself in the process. But the intent and motivation determines how you are perceived -- as a self-serving professional or as a sensitive, caring leader who brings out the best in others.

Move from Negotiation to Navigation

The very term 'negotiation' reeks of a difficult process of extracting value in return for an investment. Often it involves shadow boxing, power plays and complex gaming rules. If you are truly enlightened, you will seek to move from operating as a negotiator to a new avatar -- that of a navigator. A navigator is simply a higher form of negotiator. Instead of striving to enhance one's own spoils, a navigator takes the trouble of ensuring that the opposing party gains an equal victory. The effort to move to Navigation includes a level playing field, although in real-terms they are hardly ever level. For instance, when during the appraisal cycle, if you are a boss who is traditionally seen as a tough negotiator when it comes to your own stakes but very miserly when it comes to dishing out stuff to your subordinates, you cannot have a different set of rules. You need to apply the same set of rules that you feel are applicable to you, to your peers and subordinates as well. Much as it may seem Utopian, it is important to recognize that it is the only time of the year when such conversations happen with employees and if you short change them then, the rest of the year is spent in silent resentment or open bitterness towards the organization, mostly caused by you.

A skilful navigator is someone who identifies the stakes for all the stakeholders and strives to achieve success in equal measures. He does not move towards complete focus on achievements and lose his people. On the other hand, he does not prefer people over productivity. He navigates the complex maps of human behaviour and organizational cultures to deliver acceptable outcomes at regular intervals.

Navigators play fair

There is an undiluted commitment towards the organization's mission and personal goals. As a result, they lead from moral authority as opposed to titular power. Since they are vocal and transparent with their intent, the team rallies behind them almost with predictable energy. They are driven by the axiom – that "integrity is who you are when no one is watching" and as a result people begin to trust them implicitly, a rare luxury in a high-stakes environment. There is a delight that flows out of relationships that guarantee fairplay and where outcomes are predictable. People know they can give their full blooded effort when they are certain that they will be rewarded fairly and no one will steal their glory.

Navigators enrich the journey

Look around you, and see if there is a positive leader who inspires you. Chances are that he or she inspired you not just because that leader is an achiever, but because of a personal trait that connected with you or a goal that resonated with you. You'll bet your enthusiasm, effort and often your dreams on such leaders because they promise to take you along with them in their own quest for success. Such leaders inspire cult-like following simply because the human spirit longs to transcend the mundane. You can be such a leader, if you are willing to invest yourself in others. Not only do you rally behind such people with fervour, you replicate such a model within your own sphere of influence. This cascades to other people and the whole organisation is that much richer because someone leapt to a new paradigm.

Navigators think legacy

They know that long after their destination is reached, there lies a final destiny. While they are constantly striving to accomplish the immediate, their eyes are firmly fixed on the finish line. They know that each day, they are contributing to their legacy. Finally when someone leaves a job or a company, they may move to the new role and new location but the impact they made while they were working stays. The only question is whether it was a legacy to be cherished or eminently forgettable. When corporate epitaphs are written, often references are made to achievements but no one forgets that Character is the bedrock from which excellence springs. When the next achiever comes along and becomes the new flavour, it is one's character that defines a lasting legacy. Those navigators who lead from an unwavering set of principles that are anchored in strong character leave an indelible and memorable legacy.

Let me close with a compelling true-life incident that occurred in my own work life. A few years ago, two senior managers ganged up against me to stifle my visibility and growth opportunities. I remained cordial to them even to the point of not holding any grudges against them. In a remarkable turn around of circumstances, the very folks who were baying for my blood, ended up looking for jobs and seeking my help in getting some references within my network. Like Robert Schuller says "tough times don't last, tough people do". If I harboured negative feelings and refused to even communicate with them, I would have shut the door to this opportunity to help when they were down. There is no greater feeling of elation when it sinks in that you could have got even, but you got better. That now set the foundation for relationships that have withstood the vicissitudes of life.

Shift your focus from success to delight. A happy worker is not a contradiction in terms

Ten Popular Office Myths

No, none of these statements are true, so do a reality check now. Have you fallen prey to any of these office myths? Learn to shrug them off... and enter the real world!

1. Since I rush around all the time, I am fairly important here.
2. I am always on the phone; therefore I am quite a chap.
3. I speak the loudest and I'm always shouting for or about something; therefore everyone must think I am a hotshot executive.
4. I am always dropping names, particularly the names of those at the top; so I must be powerful too.
5. I keep track of even the minutiae in the organisation, so I am fully plugged into everything that's happens here.
6. I am the one who gets things done here. So I am indispensable to the organisation.
7. No one here bothers to do things right, except me.
8. I am the first to hear all the important news. So I am truly important.
9. I am the boss's right-hand man. If I quit supporting him, the whole department will collapse.
10. I have been here the longest. So no one knows the stuff around here better than I do.

Four Snares to Avoid While at Work

The Whiner

Always dwelling on the negative distorts your perspective and gives you a warped view of your rights and responsibilities. Pause to think for a moment: is there anyone in your organisation (and that includes you) who is guilty of griping about the pay, the bosses, the subordinates, the weather and when he can't find anything new, even about himself – his health, his family and his cat?

Such people drain the spirit because complaining is contagious. If you are not careful they will spread their infection to you, and soon you'll find your shoulders drooping and your spirits sagging. Either shower them with optimism or run for cover.

My best unsolicited advice ever: Quit griping or quit!

The 'Cheat'

People often short-change the organisation they work for because they are ungrateful or harbour a grouse. They bring their bodies to work but their minds and hearts are left back home or elsewhere. So they try to get away with contributing far less of their time, talents and energy than is required of them. They may think that they are getting away with it, but in the end it is the man in the mirror who gets cheated. If you are a cheater yourself and you cheat because you feel you are not getting your due, make a case and try to win what you deserve. Otherwise quit and go to a place that you feel will appreciate and reward you more. But if you stay in the same place and continue to cheat, you are not only robbing the organisation of your valuable contribution but also eroding your personality.

The Worrier

Are you forever worrying compulsively over even the smallest details? This deprives you of the ability to think straight and recharge yourself, so relax... the Apocalypse is coming, but it is not here yet. Give people the benefit of the doubt when they say they will do something. Breathing down their neck till their task is completed will only reduce their output and send you into a tailspin.

The 'Conqueror'

As the saying goes, honey catches more flies than vinegar, and you don't have to set out to bulldoze when you can persuade. A confrontational attitude blurs your perspective on everything, and invites retaliation. So it helps if you remember that it is not always a win-lose situation that you're faced with. As we mature at work, we begin to realise that it is important for all of us to work as genuine, respectful individuals who have come together for a cause. Learn to empathise with others and seek out their views on matters of importance to you. It is amazing how far you can go, if only you are willing to see them not as adversaries but as advocates, maybe, in a different dimension. Some of my best moments at work happened when those with whom I had had a run-in earlier and then did an about-turn after we'd had some honest and genuine exchanges.

I once attended a cocktail party with some colleagues drawn from almost all departments at work. After a few rounds – I must have been the only one in the group who was getting high on orange juice – people started to open up, and I teased a few of them by confessing that all along I had thought of them as hard nuts to crack and it had taken the casual bonhomie between all of us that evening to change my opinion of them. Surprisingly, they replied that the feeling was mutual! Earlier, they had been responsible for some tough times at work, but the right responses in the right environment had smoothed ruffled feathers and laid the foundation for lasting friendships, and even today, I keep in touch with them.

How to Rise Above Adversity at Work

What is adversity? Adversity is not rejection or defeat. If the results of an endeavour that you have participated in are not satisfactory, it may be due to downright shortfall in performance. Making lame excuses for such failures and attributing it to adversity is only a form of denial. But what if you are not imagining things and you truly are being targeted by a person or a group? Adversity is triggered by many things, some of which may be exceedingly trivial – your name, where you were born, the colour of your skin and what you look like, or your personality or designation. Since these are factors beyond your control, keep your eyes open for the stuff that you can do something about. It is important to recognise why you are being singled out for special treatment and respond accordingly. For instance, some forms of adversity, such as mild efforts to slight you, should be brushed aside.

But there are signs you should watch out for that will tell you the situation is a tad more serious. Are you repeatedly treated in a way that baffles you because it seems unfair and unreasonable? Are you not given enough chances or even if you are, is the outcome mysteriously unfavourable to you? Do you feel that you have to work extra hard to get what comes easily to others? Do you constantly find yourself pushed into situations where you end up being embarrassed? If your answer is 'Yes' to any of these questions, it's time to take action.

1. Learn When to Move On

In the hyper-competitive world of business, you'll be slain in one fell swoop if you make a single wrong move. More humiliating is the loss of face that goes with being outmanoeuvred in various games of office politics. How do you fight by playing within the rules, yet stay competitive, and let the outcome be governed by unseen forces you cannot even fathom? As the stakes get higher in the corporate ranks, it is no longer the survival of the many that matters; it is success at any cost. To get to a coveted promotion or bag a fancy project, there are many who would do whatever it takes to stake their claim. Often, it means that they will step on someone else's aspirations, ride roughshod over their colleagues' reputation, and speak disparagingly of everyone else, just to emerge as the frontrunner.

Do you find that you are repeatedly overlooked when the time comes for promotions or raises, even though your performance merits both? Do you feel as if you are caught in a snare, while your peers are racing ahead? The chances are that you are a victim of career oppression. There are some managers who project themselves in a blaze of glory and completely eclipse the work of their teams. Unfortunately, those at the top also continue to reward such leaders although they never take their colleagues or subordinates along with them.

In such a scenario, you really are trapped. Or, you might have an inflated view of your work, in which case the perceived persecution may not be true. But if you get good ratings each year, it is possible that your boss may be blocking your career path. Frankly, very few organisations are equipped to handle such conflicts. You may be stuck because you are scared of intensifying the problem by complaining about the deadlock to higher authorities. Or, you may not want to be seen as a cry baby by other senior leaders. This is a classic situation that many employees face because the hierarchy itself does not offer any solution to such issues.

Frankly, nothing works better than opting to move, particularly if you are a star performer. At that point, others might jump in to pacify you, but then, as you would instinctively know, it is a bit too late in the day for any peace-brokering. Usually, the biggest source of adversity is a boss.

And therein lies the rub. The relationship you share with your boss can determine whether your workplace is a living hell or a paradise, for he can either harness your abilities or hamper your progress. The role of a boss is akin to that of a coach. And bosses are, by and large, responsible for their team performing like a well-oiled machine or a rickety, cranky set of wheels.

Not all forms of adversity stem from external sources. If you make an honest and ruthless assessment of your performance, the chances are you will discover some of the mistakes committed, perhaps unwittingly, by you. You may be inclined to overlook all your errors, but the colleagues, bosses and others who have had to bear the brunt of your mistakes will keep them tucked away in their elephantine memories and pay you back with interest. Make no mistake, what you sow comes back to haunt you or help you. A careless remark or a delayed response can be taken as a slight and when it's payback time, it can hurt. You'll be amazed how petty some folks can be, just to get even. Often, they trample upon you not only to teach you a lesson but also to instil the fear of god in the onlookers, lest others make a similar mistake. With such people, be on your guard all the time. Sure, this contradicts my earlier tip that you should let your guard down and build relationships, but then, there are exceptions to every rule. In this case, the moment you let your guard down, you are also setting yourself up to be exploited, for a clever manipulator knows how to extract information from others and use it for his own ends.

2. Gain the Right Perspective

Whether you are the aggrieved party or the aggressor, it is important to gain a healthy perspective. What if instead of sulking when you feel you have been treated unfairly, you adopt a neutral attitude and seek feedback from the source of aggression? What if instead of using your power to withhold rewards, you counsel, frankly and maturely, the employee who may have erred? Would such responses benefit your organisation, or would you be serving it better by taking off on your personal power trips?

An important factor that will help you gain the right perspective is the realisation that everyone is there to serve a larger organisation. Aligning yourself to the vision and mission of the organisation helps both the warring parties to submit to a higher authority without feeling that they have lost face. How can the organisation benefit from the unique skills and talents you bring to the table, if one of you is not contributing wholeheartedly to its progress? People come and go but organisations are 'going entities', and surely there is room for both of you to leave an indelible impression in the corridors of your organisation.

Another way to gain a proper perspective is by taking on the hat of a coach. If you were coaching someone in a different setting, say, within the family, or in the community, would you still get locked into win-lose positions? Or I-am-right-therefore-you-are-wrong stances? Some of the harsh, ruthless managers at work turn into tender-hearted, compassionate individuals the moment they step out of the office and it invariably works wonders for them. So why suppress the finer emotions during work hours?

3. Be Ready to Embrace Change

As Heraclitus said, 'You cannot step into the same river twice.' Sure, it's a cliché that change is the new order, but that's the truth! In fact, it is through change that we who live in this brave new world survive. But for most of us, change is worrying and disruptive and usually unwelcome. We would much rather stick with the status quo even though we grumble about it. But since change is inevitable, how best can we cope with it?

a. Float and Flow

Look around you and recollect what life was like barely three or even five years ago. You will be astonished at the rapidity with which change has enveloped us. Survivors recognise the inexorable nature of this tidal wave, and instead of resisting it, they reach out to change, and proactively ride the new wave. Instead of the traditional fight-or-flight responses, they adopt the third option of float-and-flow. Sometimes, they go underwater and stay submerged for a while, but they resurface again because they understand the dynamics of change, and let it work in their favour.

b. Expect the Unexpected

First of all, survivors never lose sight of the adage 'expect the unexpected'. They understand what it means to have a fire drill, to simulate the conditions of real-life scenarios and play their mental tapes over and over again. 'What can go wrong?' is a question they ask not only themselves but also their mentors, their subordinates, and their well-wishers till they have multiple valid responses that they sift and fine-tune to arrive at the best damage-control solutions.

c. Face Change with Detachment

Survivors have mastered the ability of staying detached and even dispassionate during moments of change, and its accompanying upheavals. The resilient ones know that deep down they have the wherewithal to not get worked up when stuff happens to them and around them. Because they have simulated such experiences so many times, an automatic response kicks in and their locus of control is hardly affected. (Management text books define someone's 'locus of control' as a state of equilibrium that gets disrupted when external stimuli or events cause change.) In professional situations, high stress occurs during mergers and acquisitions or when a new boss takes over. In personal life, there are many equally serious life-changing events that one has to embrace without completely falling apart.

d. Wait, Watch, Act

Because survivors have been through a series of high-stress events, and their mesh of experience has sieved many such episodes, they are able to draw enough energy from their mental reserves to condition themselves. They watch and wait, carefully calibrating their response because they know the right time to speak or act. In the moment of reckoning, they act purposefully because they are confident that their response will be appropriate. They make excellent catalysts because they have the experience to anticipate changes long before others are aware of any such possibilities. Change is a fact of life; so embrace it, for positioning yourself as an agent of change is a sure way of demonstrating a resilient spirit, a precondition for success in today's world.

4. Be Resilient and Bounce Back Boldly

The Chinese word for crisis has two meanings – 'danger' and 'opportunity'. A hopeful, resilient and optimistic individual looks at each crisis as an opportunity to become better, to test himself against the elements and live to tell the tale. Those who are resilient are always pushing themselves out of their comfort zone to do what needs to be done.

From childhood we are taught to stay safe, live responsibly, and not do anything reckless – on such paradigms of safety and comfort are we encouraged to build our lives. These ideas subsequently become fetters or pegs that hold us back in our quest for growth and freedom. 'Don't take too many risks,' is what we are constantly told. But everyone knows that the higher an individual's risk-taking capability, the greater the rewards. We are not meant to live in a comfort zone. The distant dreams and the horizon always beckon the spirit of the voyager within.

I am not for a moment suggesting that we shirk our responsibilities and take completely outrageous steps but I am advocating fearless, confident forays to grasp opportunities that lie just outside our comfort zone. Each time I moved to a different city, it meant uprooting myself, my relationships and whatever I was comfortable with to start life all over again. I have moved five cities and seven homes over the last twelve years. In return, the rich tapestry of experience I was able to weave, not just for myself but for my family and my colleagues, was worth the effort. Perhaps, I wouldn't have had such a wide repertoire of experiences had I just stayed within my comfort zone, in my hometown. Just as conquering physical spaces expands your personality, you stretch your mind and spirit when you leave the confines of familiarity in search of novel experiences. No wonder kings used to send their princes to the outermost reaches of their kingdom as part of their growing-up experience. Because once you traverse a territory, the road becomes a part of you. You carry the landscape with you as it becomes stamped on your soul.

Resilient people have an unlimited capacity to handle ambiguity. Paradoxical it may seem but resilient people have a disciplined approach towards managing ambiguity. They build their approach on clues, on previous experiences and a deep rooted confidence. Their can-do attitude allows them to show up in completely new situations and emerge with a positive result. They have an intuitive grasp of how things ought to work, and they also have an-built capacity to process exceptions.

In the IT industry where I make a living, for the past decade or so, I have been an onlooker at the scene of a fascinating discipline called PROCESS. Depending on the person you talk to, the word process can elicit two equally intense but opposing reactions. One is an absolute infatuation with the word and the other, contempt and disgust. Those who love it, embrace it because processes make teams, individuals and organisations predictable and paves the way for precise work. Those who loathe it do so because processes reduce work into measurable units and leave out creativity and wonder. Most processes are well thought out and work with clock like precision. But the moment a process breaks down, all those who were enslaved by the process now have to deal with ambiguity and thus manage stress.

Those who run teams by the seat of their pants 'or management by the butt' find it difficult to embrace processes or subject themselves to the discipline that processes impose. Resilient individuals have a remarkable capacity to work with processes but also deal with the unexpected with equal élan. They actually show results when processes break down and everyone is scurrying for a response. A rigid adherence to predictable processes makes one an automaton and a total disregard for it could lead to anarchy. The resilient one finds the right balance, for as the ancient proverb goes: A wise man avoids all extremes.

Resilient people are more journey-oriented than destination-driven. Detours, setbacks and the occasional breakdowns do not deter a resilient individual. In fact, they celebrate the occasion by stopping to smell the roses on the way. They even welcome the occasional change of plan because they see only the silver lining in every dark cloud. They have a high wonder quotient and are willing to spend time looking at rocks, flora and fauna along the way. Because of their sense of wonder, everything they see is a fascinating miracle. So even in a crisis, while everyone is counting the losses, they look for the gains, if any, and strive to move on to the next milestone. No wonder such people make wonderful travel companions with their zest for life and positive disposition and cheer which inspires others as they trudge along. And they remind us of the truth that the journey is often as important as the destination.

Ten Immutable Laws of Visibility

Another way in which adversity commonly manifests itself is in the form of a boss or colleague who pushes you to the background and takes the credit for your painstaking work. So how do you stay visible?

Well, it all starts on day one. Your visibility commences right from the time you walk in through the door and make your way softly to the reception. You are being watched, and albeit subtly, people notice the way you reach out and introduce yourself to everyone. How confident are you? Do you just mumble a few words and run to your desk? Or do you walk as if you have worked there for a long time?

You'll never get a second chance to make a first impression. In fact, a former colleague of mine even today makes fun of the very first time I walked into the office for my interview. As my potential boss was insistent on meeting me at the earliest occasion possible, I chose to attend the job interview shortly after my sister's wedding that afternoon. Overdressed as I was, I had apparently caused quite a stir! Now ask your colleagues to describe their first impression of you, and you'll be surprised at how vividly they remember your entry into the organisation. If you want to make an impact, ensure that you carry yourself well.

1. Be Natural

Even at work when you are looking for ways to impress, you don't have to keep building your image all the time. The best impression you can make is by being yourself. Carry your most cheerful self to work. That does not mean you should be casual about everything, but just show that you are comfortable with yourself. Such a relaxed demeanour draws others to you. If you are secure in yourself you may even be able to change the behaviour of the people around you. There will be those who are grumpy, there will be others who, like Atlas, seem to carry the weight of the world on their shoulders. But you ought to be as natural as possible, because any artificiality will be exposed, sooner or later. Be genuine, be yourself. In the long run, you won't have to pretend to be somebody you are not.

2. Be Humble

If there is one quality that I see conspicuously absent, it is humility. Unless you work in a hospital, it is never a matter of life and death, although everyone wants us to believe that it is. So take the time to reach out to everyone who crosses your path. Be open, be friendly and share with them a moment or two, and who knows, you may be enriching them or be enriched by them. Where you are in the hierarchy of the organisation is not important, it is what you are as a person that makes an impression on others. The hierarchy is just a structure to get work done in the organisation. Just because you are either a big shot or close to one doesn't make you any different from a junior colleague. Build relationships, you'll be richer in every sense of the term.

3. Learn to Shine

There is a difference between applauding yourself and giving your best to everything, at every possible opportunity, and shining in the process. Often, people mistake one for the other. Unless your job demands utmost secrecy, you ought to be visible on every possible occasion. Meet people across teams and departments, and never make the mistake of allowing yourself to be pigeon-holed in a team or designation. I am not advocating that you move away from your core work and start networking around the organisation without any purpose. But at every meeting or gathering you should either contribute your mite or be seen actively engaging with other stakeholders. Even if all it does is to pave the way for brief encounters with the 'top guns', it is worth the effort. Be attentive and keenly interested in what they have to offer. If you have a well-thought-out opinion, do share it with them. If you can make your presence felt at the meeting by asking questions or suggesting ideas do it in such a way that it leaves an impression.

4. Pick the Difficult Projects

If you want to outshine the rest and make a name for yourself, find out about the toughest, biggest or even the most crucial projects that are critical to the organisation's success. Of course, every department views its role and its projects as vital, but there is a hierarchy in every company and if the effects of your contribution can be felt in the top departments crucial to the company, then you are guaranteed visibility. Remember, this is a long-term game and you don't want to be seen as a blazing star, but as a steady performer who is there to perform for many seasons. At the early stages of your career, the cowboy approach may help, but those who dig deep and plant themselves well are the ones who are likely to be seen as top-notch leaders.

5. Map the Movers and Shakers

Success is never a solitary achievement. It is the result of several forces including powerful allies. During the early stages of your sojourn in an organisation, you can cleverly ride on your past reputation. Within a year or two, you ought to have built your reputation in the current organisation. Constantly refer to your own goals and desires that are in sync with those of the key allies you want to build, as you spend time in the organisation. However, always remember the responses you draw from them will be dependent on your boss. So you need to pay attention to your boss's reputation and draw your plans accordingly. If your boss or leader has had serious disagreements with all and sundry, then you need to carve a niche for yourself as he is likely to impede, not help.

6. Always Seek Advice from Others

Every top executive invariably has a passion or hobby that he would love to talk about at length. You'll not only get some valuable free advice but also get closer to the executives in those precious moments you get to spend with them. Of course, you will be able to approach them only after a protracted period of time, but it is worth the effort. Over the years, I have benefited from the savvy investment ideas of some of the senior executives I have met and spent time with. Such people are high achievers with a wealth of experience and it is available for the smart ones who can tap it cleverly. They have reached where they are now because they have something in them. Only the cynics think otherwise, and no one ever gets close to a cynic. When we ask someone for advice it is tacitly understood that we look up to them, and there is something about the human spirit that enjoys being lifted up to that level. And even if you don't end up following their advice, you would have gained a different perspective of things.

7. Give Something Unique to Your Organisation

Are you an expert in some unusual area? Like astronomy, or maybe even something esoteric? This is your chance to shine by organising a brief lecture or a demonstration in your area of expertise. You don't have to be famous or an acclaimed authority to contribute. Tie it to some occasion like World Environment Day if the topic lends itself to that sort of thing, and you are bound to stand out if you are seen to be championing a cause or focusing on some vital area that affects everyone. A friend of mine was involved in a bike accident and broke his hand, but fortunately his life was saved because he wore a helmet. Shortly after he recovered, he began a crusade to raise people's awareness of the need to wear helmets to stay safe. Even though he was shy and reserved, his personal interest in the safety of bike riders catapulted him into the limelight, initially in the organisation where he worked and then way beyond that. Other companies and social organisations started to invite him to speak and raise their employees' awareness of the topic. The traffic police department also joined hands with him later in making it a citywide campaign. Such is the impact of an individual who backs himself to contribute something worthwhile, and what starts with baby steps can become a large movement.

8. Connect People Wherever Possible

You can raise your personal visibility if you are seen as a 'connector'. Most denizens of the corporate world want to hold on to their contacts and information and never share either, unless it benefits them in some way. If you offer to help bring people together and do so without a selfish agenda, even if the offer is not taken up, they will remember that you went out of your way to make such an offer.

9. Reach Out to People in Need

You will find that many families are battling with sickness or the needs for their children or whatever, and with extended families on the way out, they do not always have people with whom they can share their problems. Be ready to lend a shoulder, ask around, and proactively suggest courses of action that are likely to be helpful. The fact that you took the trouble of thinking through the problem with them is reassuring to the ones to whom you offer help. A friend or colleague who stood by them is not forgotten in a hurry, and kindness always has a boomerang effect.

10. Get Involved in Causes that Your Organisation Supports

There is no better way to network with your colleagues than in a joint effort to change the world. In this day and age when corporate social responsibility is at an all time high, it is easy to plug into the official networks. Usually, these causes have sponsorship and buy-in at the highest level, so it is imperative for you to be a part of this activity. Not only will you get a chance to meet high-powered executives in an informal atmosphere, but you can also go on to mention in your resume how it made a difference to your own life. Above all, using some of your time and energy for a cause lifts your spirit. My current employer is a big sponsor of marathons around the world. Now that I am a convert to the 'cult' of long-distance running, I take immense pride in sharing with others how my company helped me hone my new-found passion. And since it all sounds so natural and what comes through, strong and clear is the passion I feel when I talk of my interest in running and so very few people think that I am plugging my company. So even when I post anything about my organisation on Facebook or in my personal websites, it flows from a genuine sense of ownership and does not sound contrived.

Sixteen Smart Steps to Boost Your Confidence

Self-confidence is one of the key factors that will help you stay visible, and here are some handy hints to shore it up:

1. Know that you don't have to know it all – nobody does!
2. Why worry constantly about what others think of you? What matters is what you think of yourself.
3. Do everything deliberately, because you want to, and not because you have to.
4. Know what makes you uniquely, distinctly, YOU.
5. Know your hot buttons and cold buttons.
6. Don't be apologetic about everything you do. Do your best and look the world fearlessly in the face.
7. Trust your feelings.
8. Hold on to your ideals.
9. Look to your past to determine the present.
10. Know your cheerleaders and your coach, and separate them from the spectators.
11. Keep learning.
12. Dig deeper into your inner strength at each stage of your journey, and help others along the way.
13. Give yourself pep talks – incessantly. No one can encourage you better than yourself.
14. Recall your original dream.

15. Then ask yourself, 'What is my next milestone on the journey?'

16. Find what gives you a rush and pursue it with passion.

To sum up

To conclude, let me share with you the words of one my favourite singers, with whom I share my middle name, Bob Dylan:

"I ain't lookin' to compete with you
Beat or cheat or mistreat you
Simplify you, classify you
Deny, defy or crucify you
All I really want to do
Is, baby, be friends with you"

CHAPTER 7

From Chump to Champ

If you're a champion, you have to have it in your heart.

– Chris Evert

Whenever our ad agency was asked to pitch for business, if it meant handling a product in the marketplace, we would undertake to perform what is known as a brand audit. Through this fairly comprehensive exercise, we would learn how a brand is perceived by the various stakeholders – existing customers, potential customers, people using other products in the same category, et al… This exercise always helped us arrive at a picture of the various perceptions of the product. Likewise, if you were to undertake a brand audit exercise of yourself, what would you learn?

Do a Brand Audit to Find the Real You

No brand can become a preferred brand if it does not consciously evolve in its journey. What do your colleagues say about you? What does their top-of-the-mind recall indicate? What do they say are some of your key traits – are they in agreement with what you yourself have to say about the brand called YOU? If there is a large gap between what others feel or say about you and your own opinion of yourself, then your assessment needs to be calibrated, so that you know who and what you really are. For without knowing the product – yourself, in this case – you cannot pitch it to others, whether it is your management, colleagues or even future employers.

So where can you begin? Well, if you have a Linkedin Profile, what recommendations do you have and what are the common denominators in those recommendations that people mirrored back to you?

In management circles, one of the aphorisms that you hear is: *Potential is recognised but performance is rewarded*. You might be recruited because you demonstrate potential, but what keeps you going each year is what you've clocked up during the entire appraisal cycle. In fact, each appraisal can be viewed as a brand audit of sorts as some of the key stakeholders like your supervisor and your big boss can convey in words their perception of your work during the year. Often, if there is not too much of a gap between the assessments made by you and the powers-that-be, you are rewarded financially.

But you don't have to wait for the year-end verdict to decode the way you are perceived by the people around you. What are the signals that people send out when you deal with them? Do you sense their confidence in you, or does a feeling of uncertainty or apathy come through? In the corporate world, apathy is far worse than antipathy. If you are being treated with indifference, then you are no longer a force to reckon with, and you need to reorient your style. Here are some smart strategies you can adopt at work.

1. Speak the Right Language

Whenever a request is made by someone at the workplace, what is your instant response? Are you watchful, cautious and measured in what you say, or do you extend an enthusiastic invitation to work together? I once worked with a brash, 'cowboy' colleague, who had the reputation of being a bully. However, the first time he met me, he was unusually cordial and when he was looking for some information, I volunteered to help him. Then he blurted out that he had been told by others that I would willingly go the extra mile to be helpful and it had made him favourably disposed towards me even before we had ever met. Remember your reputation precedes you. And whether you make or mar your reputation is singularly dependent on you.

Even if there is a need to respond cautiously to someone's request for your participation in some area of work, the manner in which you respond can still lead to a positive outcome. Most people in an organisation are reasonable, intelligent people who want to advance their careers. As long as you take a respectful view of that, everyone around will warm up to you. However, if you ignore everyone's agenda except yours, then you are likely to develop the reputation of being self-centred. That approach might work on a short-term basis but, in the long run, it is bound to be counter-productive.

2. Be in Sync with the Larger Picture

It is always important to be in alignment with your team, department and organisation's goals. It is the boss's prerogative to set the priorities, but ensuring that you and your work are fully synchronized with the larger picture can help you go places. Often, young professionals adopt a short-sighted approach without realising that their work is interlinked with that of the other teams and ultimately affects the success of the organisation. Only professionals with a holistic perspective emerge as leaders because they can view their work and the team's roles in the right context.

3. Root Out Those Blind Spots

Often what you don't know can really hurt you. One of the most frustrating elements in corporate life is the mysterious, often unknown mechanism by which one gets promotions and rewards. Despite doing everything you could possibly do, often it is someone else who gets the nod for a promotion that you so fittingly deserve or atleast think you deserve. You could cry foul, feel contemptuous of the other guy for sucking up to the boss. Maybe you could come up with a number of uncharitable excuses, but there must have been some X-factor that tilted the balance in his favour. No one is ever promoted on capability alone. The individual also needs to be savvy enough to work the organisational hierarchy.

If you find that you are missing the bus all too often, seek mentoring and get genuine, dispassionate feedback so that even if you decide to move to another organisation, you will be aware of your Achilles heel and hopefully do something about it, so as to position yourself firmly to grab the next opportunity. Your previous success could end up as a blind spot. Not crediting your teams adequately can create obstacles that handicap you. If you are not willing to invest in yourself and make the time and effort required to keep abreast of things and learn constantly, it can impede your growth. Maturity is hard to define but easy to spot in someone, simply because it is strikingly conspicuous. So keep your head at all times. Those who are around you might appear to be congenial but each word, each action is constantly being tucked away in someone's memory. When it's payback time, you will be surprised to find that your unwitting errors have boomeranged to haunt you. A fancy term called 360 degree feedback is now doing the rounds in corporate circles, whereby all those around you – customers, partners, subordinates, supervisors and peers – are being asked to rate and evaluate you. Such a rounded approach helps remove a person's blind spots. Brilliant professionals are constantly ahead of the learning curve not just by being up to date with the latest information available, but also by smartly applying the lessons learnt in inter-personal situations. In fact, most organisations place a premium on such leaders who are seasoned enough to navigate thorny, politically-charged environments.

4. Don't Let Speed Bumps Deter You

There are times when even your best efforts cannot conjure up a positive outcome, and those affected will be disappointed with you. But if you almost always do your best and deliver the goods, and stay focused on ensuring that all interactions are satisfactorily concluded, most people are happy to let you get on with accomplishing what you have set out to do. Of course, there will be bumps along the way, which you would need to ride over, but then, you already know that!

5. Don't Get on the High Horse

Sometimes, you might run into invisible walls and find that you and your work get stuck at that point. Perhaps, someone doesn't like you or your boss or your team, but whatever the reason, that someone doesn't deem your work important enough to give it some attention. When you run into a stone wall, it is safe to assume that there is an 'issue', most likely a relationship breakdown. Till you uncover the real problem, you will be dealing with smokescreens that are set up to distract, obfuscate and stall progress. The information provided will be scanty, if at all. You will have to repeatedly ask for the smallest of things, and when the person is confronted, it is likely to blow up into a major showdown, and the real issue would still not have been addressed. In times like these, take a deep breath and get out of the normal 'process' of doing business. Stop dashing off emails and pick up the phone. If phones don't work, get face time. If they are still elusive, then think hard. Sometimes, there may be a genuine reason that can't be disclosed by the other side, but do give them the benefit of doubt in the interest of the relationship. If you get stuck on your 'right' they will be forced to choose what is 'left'. In the end, you will find that you have painted yourself into a corner, and might never be able to conduct your business with them again on the same footing.

6. Expand Your 'Awareness Spectrum'

In small organisations, it is easy to get acquainted with everyone you need to interact with in the conduct of your business. In large organisations you might need to ride on your boss's visibility and methodically build a track record for yourself. So how do you make people aware of you? First of all, your ability to become visible is directly proportional to your dynamism. Being dynamic doesn't mean rolling around like a loose cannon. It means purposefully investing your efforts in high visibility activity. For example, every company has its own Intranet – a web portal that allows employees to interact with one another. You need to be present within such forums and start engaging with others. For example, there are contests that are run, and articles – both in technical areas and of general interest – are regularly solicited. So contribute to these forums in some way, and if you are constantly being seen as a creative individual with clever opinions, then you are making ripples in the right circles. You ought to utilise every avenue available to enhance your presence. Once you are published, start circulating those pieces around to your colleagues who may not have seen them on the Intranet.

7. Map the 'Connectors' and 'High Network' Individuals

When you walk into an organisation, remember that every employee can make a difference to your work. In every organisation there are many individuals whose influence is disproportionately larger than their designation seems to merit. If you strictly follow the organisational hierarchy, then you'll make the mistake of looking only at the top of the pyramid. However, there are many who are spread along the base of the pyramid whose influence pans across the organisation. For example, the 'gatekeepers' of the powerful bosses are typically very influential in an invisible manner. These silent players can often make a tremendous difference to those who work well with them. A librarian in one of the organisations where I had worked in the past was a good example of this. She was the one who would alert me that certain books dealing with my area of expertise had been ordered and were on the way. She not only saved me money because some of those books were on my 'to buy' list, but also brought to my notice several other relevant articles and clippings on the subject, as well as various job opportunities abroad. All because we shared a cordial working relationship...

Another reason you want to pay attention to such employees is that they are often underappreciated in their roles. Typically, those in support roles in administrative areas are great enablers of business but because they are not directly generating revenue or visibility, they are often eclipsed by more high profile departments such as sales, marketing, finance and so on... It is easy to be cordial and friendly with someone who is part of your circle of work on a regular basis. But what is of crucial importance is that you create your reputation by aligning yourself with everyone. You'll be so much richer for those friendships, more so if you make it evident that you value their inherent worth as much as their professional contribution.

Pre-wiring your network helps you create a buzz long before you harness the airwaves. Don't let the task or goal at hand become larger than life and consume everything else. It is important that you understand and keep in perspective what drives each individual. See people in that context of their families, hobbies, passions and interests for all these add up to make the individual. It helps if you don't have any ulterior motive, other than to just work well and enrich each other.

Influence doesn't come from power. Influence comes from connections. If you are stuck in your cubicle like a rabbit in a burrow, you'll never be able to create or harness relationships. Influence comes from circulation. A rolling stone does gather 'mass'.

* * *

Think Like a Champion!

Now, let's assume that you have acted on these tips and adopted a slew of smart strategies at work. So what would help you ensure that all of these come together to bring you the success and the accolades that you have been hoping for? Well, to be a 'champion' on the sports field or at the workplace, you need to think like a champion and act like one. Did you say, 'But how does one do that?' Then read on...

Acquire a Champion's Mindset

Connecting with people across the organisation is no easy task. You need to traverse many lines, including 'enemy lines'! Also, there may be times when you find you can depend on no one except yourself as you soldier on, for those who should bat with you – your boss and your team – may be the primary players who inhibit your progress. Or there might be prickly power equations among the top brass, and they might even try to manipulate you to suit their agendas. Never get cowed down by those in authority. Use their power to your advantage by treating them all with equal attention and respect, and make sure that you are a 'value-add' whichever 'faction' you are working with at any given point.

What Is the Pay-Off?

Since those in power usually have any number of sycophants milling around them, someone who is respectful and ever willing to pitch in when needed but does not toady to them, comes across as a refreshing change. Such a healthy attitude creates a sense of mutual respect, and when you deal with the rich and the powerful without grovelling, they begin to treat you with more respect than they would their seemingly blind devotees who apparently worship the very ground they walk on. There is mistaken notion that 'apple polishers' always go places. Like most myths there is an element of truth in it, but it is not always the case. The astute, experienced leaders who run companies or institutions also possess the judgement to distinguish between those who say the right things to get some benefit for themselves and those with whom the overall good of the organisation comes first.

Champions Live by Their Convictions

At a superficial level, your principles and convictions might appear to be stumbling blocks in the path of your success. Not so! In fact, living by your convictions is a prerequisite to being able to live with yourself, and unless you can do that, how can you function at your peak professionally or in any other area? But what if your values clash with those of others who may be in positions of power? Can you reconcile diametrically different viewpoints and ensure that you are able to function effectively? Yes, you can, and I have first-hand experience of this as you will see. There is no greater joy than being known as the 'go to' person when large tasks or projects come the team's way, for it shows that, slowly, your leadership is beginning to take root.

In every team there will be folks who are the primary

movers and shakers, and there are the rest who diligently implement the tasks. Depending on where you want to emerge in the team, you need to calibrate your influence and impact. There is also a general belief that as you advance in your own career path, you'll gain leadership. Not entirely true. As the industry matures and more and more folks join the work-place, or when opportunities diminish in the light of growing competition, it is only those who adeptly manage across teams (that often compete) that rise to leadership. Do look out for the trends that are impacting your organisation. You'll need to position yourself to ride the wave whenever the timing is right.

But remember that the battle is not always won by the swift or the strong. The corporate journey is more like a marathon than a sprint, remember! Hence, patience, pacing and planning are the keys to long-term success. If you enjoy the adrenaline rush and short-term bursts of a sprint, it is likely that you could spend yourself far too quickly, and soon find yourself poised on the brink of a burnout.

If you have a natural proclivity to change organisations quickly and you are uncomfortable staying in one position or organisation for a long time. Sure, there are some creative industries buzzing with such opportunities, would be ideal for folks with such a temperament. But in normal circumstances, while functioning in an organisation whose culture is governed by a conventional mindset, you would need to acquire patience in a hurry. Moreover, the stage at which you are in your career should play a major role in determining your outlook.

My outlook was impacted by the fact that I began working when I was still a teenager. I am sure some of my more 'experienced' colleagues found me naïve and brash because I tried to live up to certain ideals and made no bones about it. No matter what they said about the ways of the world and about making adjustments and compromises, I struggled to do things my way. Some challenges were particularly difficult to surmount, for early in my career I had made certain commitments to myself. For instance, I was determined never to bribe any government official to close a deal. I was in sales and had to interact with government owned companies, so that was certainly not a reasonable position to take, particularly since I had annual sales quotas. For many years I was caught in this conflict between reality and my ideals. There were times when a deal hinged on a bribe or 'gift', and I was prepared to lose the business rather than compromise my principles. But my seniors at my workplace invariably stepped in and saved the day for me, although such sales were not chalked up to my credit. But I did not mind – the job was done (and there were always other jobs without such hazards) and whoever clinched the deal and got the credit felt he owed me one. I was passionate about sales and winning financial incentives by reaching my targets, but unlike some of the others who were desperate for success, I knew that there were certain things I would never do to accomplish those goals.

Believe me, I did not lose out because of this... something else always came along, which I was more comfortable doing. And this was partly because I had dug my well before I was thirsty and had built an excellent rapport with my colleagues long before I needed their help. They were mildly annoyed with what they saw as my needless tilting at windmills, but they helped out anyway, more so because their part in the deal often involved doing something that they found enjoyable. For instance, whenever any instrumentation buyer from a government office visited our factory for inspection, there was always an expectation that he would be wined and dined at the company's expense. I enjoyed the 'dining' part because they were entertained mostly in upscale, top-of-the line restaurants, but it was the 'wining' that caused me considerable stress. Because of my convictions, I had sworn that I would never consume alcohol or smoke as I felt it would defile my body and spirit. But I was soon faced with an occupational hazard – some of the clients I entertained insisted that I, as the host, should drink with them. During such times, I would beg and plead with my colleagues to step in for me, and they willingly came to my rescue! After a while, many of those business associates realised how strong my convictions were, and began to respect the choices I had made. But it was a hard fought battle.

Some of the sales parties were a riot. I can think of countless times when I dropped my inebriated colleagues home because they were too sloshed to drive. Also, there were times when they were high and would gang up against me and try to force me to consume at least one drink. But I discovered that I could get away with it by dropping the nuclear bomb I had tucked away in my arsenal – all that I had to say was that I didn't drink for religious reasons and they would back away respectfully!

When you live for a mission, you are empowered and your dynamism radiates through every pore of your being. Yes, there are the glib talkers, who speak the right words and know how to manoeuvre political equations, but they do not have the substance or the staying power of the champion. So you can silently sneak up on them and catch them by surprise. Concede an early lead, and make way for them to get ahead. They will run out of speed and tricks because their foundation and their 'training' is faulty. You now have the advantage of the right strategies and can overtake and outlast them. It is now time for you to turn on the heat and the energy. In the corporate environment, you can win the race by creating momentum for yourself with your focus and expertise in the subject matter. You can take a different path and outmanoeuvre them, by coming up with something substantial that sets you apart.

Champions Think Out of the Box

Champions welcome and accept the unexpected even if they appear in the guise of problems, and find innovative solutions for them. In my own case, my career has taken many unexpected twists and turns and shapes – it has spanned sales, advertising, marketing and corporate communications – and I took the good and the difficult in my stride, and tried to play the game differently --my way, if you will! Let me share with you a couple of my stories.

During my days in advertising, I was given a couple of

moribund accounts that had bogged down several accounts managers who had served the agency. One of these clients was a large government company that treated us with scant respect. As a result, getting our payments from this organisation had become a nightmare, and being assigned to this account was the last step before the account manager was either sacked or left voluntarily. So I examined the track records of the account managers who had dealt with this account before. Most of them were 'tie-and-suit-wearing MBA types' or young ladies who were from top-of-the-line, 'convent' schools. When they walked into the finance department of this government office, it was a clash of two worlds. The officers there were smug, lackadaisical and laid-back whereas the MBA types were aggressive, dynamic go-getters. While the latter had all the time in the world for endless discussions over cups of tea, the MBA guys were like cowboys in cars, ready to swoop in, shoot and leave. Every time, the finance manager would just throw them out of his office within minutes, politely assuring them that the money would be paid 'soon', but that 'soon' never came.

I knew I had to think of some paradigm shifts if I wanted to tackle this account successfully. If I went by the book, I was sure to meet with as much success as my dynamic predecessors! To make a difference, I realised that I had to stop speaking in English and switched to the local language in order to bond with some of the managers. Secondly, I had to invest much more time on this project. So, instead of charging in and out like a cowboy, I opted for the shepherd's approach of hanging around the forests.

Since I was prepared to wait long hours in the finance department, I began to acquaint myself with everyone there including the head of finance, a notoriously competent, no-nonsense man who spoke in chaste Telugu. It was here that my own love for Telugu saved the day. Occasionally, I would crack jokes with these officers and even comment on any random topic so as to get close to them. After a year or so, I became so close to the finance officer that even before I had finished my hellos, he would say, 'Okay, you can come and collect a payment in the next week or so...' And the times when he said he couldn't pay, I graciously backed down and let him have his way; so that he knew that I would never try to overstep my boundaries and hustle him, but wait patiently for him to act at his convenience. The tough nut had cracked and not because I had done something extraordinary – I had played his game patiently and it had paid rich dividends. My reputation at the agency soared, for not only was I able to collect debts that were long overdue but was also able to predict to our head office, with a fair amount of accuracy, when certain collections could be made.

Pretty soon, I was able to revive the account and we had a steady stream of revenue. I knew I was a 'champion' when some of the employees at the government office enquired about my marriage plans and offered to introduce me to families that were looking for a suitable bridegroom! At which point I promptly asked my boss to remove me from that account.

The second story concerns an account in the printing

industry. My understanding of this field was zero, but I had been taken in by the paradigm that if you wear a tie and speak sophisticated English, you'll get by. Not true. Within a few months, the bankruptcy of my knowledge in that area was exposed, and I was mercilessly humiliated by a bully who was the production manager there, and couldn't stand the sight of me. I assumed that he hated me for being an MBA type who knew nothing about the hard realities of print production. But I had one thing going for me... wherever I went I would build relationships before I needed them, and that was what I had done when I'd met Radhika, who was the front office executive in a large printing press. Her best friend Joe, the production manager, was the cat's whiskers in the entire gamut of printing as he not only had a degree but also a sound knowledge of the printing press and its operations.

Between the two of them, they agreed to give me a hands-on overview of the entire production cycle in the printing industry. And they did – right from artwork to colour separation of films to plate making and printing, to post-production techniques – the whole shebang! Within a few weeks, I walked into the client's production area and, as usual, the bully told me to see him after a month. When I deconstructed his arguments in front of the whole production team, he flew into a rage and assured me that he would see me sacked. Calmly, I explained to him that if he could not take up this assignment, I would arrange to get the entire assignment completed without any help from him... and that did the trick!

Champions Assert Themselves

I have met several folks who are functionally strong and reasonably smart but are constantly quivering with fear. Their inability to speak confidently hinders their growth and day-to-day interaction with their colleagues and bosses as well. In fact, they are so overwhelmed in a social setting that, given a chance, they'd rather go back to their desk or computer and bury themselves in work. It is as if an invisible stake has been driven near their desk or computer and the further away they move, the more lost they seem to get. Their talent never gets a chance to be exhibited to others because they never stand up to be counted. Team meetings are a torture for them because they shudder at the prospect of being asked to speak or respond to a question. All their hard work is beneficial to the team leader who is only too keen to have such doormats on his team, more so as they cannot bring themselves to say 'no' to anything. In fact, since everyone around them benefits from such behaviour, often no one is motivated to point out how dysfunctional it is. But if you have slipped into such a groove, it is time to extricate yourself right now, for you are the only loser here! How? By learning to assert yourself! Assertiveness begins with a strong sense of self-respect and self-worth, and you don't have to be loud, bold or brash to be assertive. Some of the strongest champions are soft-spoken and never overbearing or given to outbreaks of hysterics.

Begin small. Start by doing what you want to do, and practise saying 'no' to certain things, firmly and without raising your voice. Initially, do this in informal settings and once you generate enough confidence in yourself, make this a part of your character. Last but not least, learn to communicate effectively and confidently. (Flip back to Chapter 2 to find out how to do this painlessly, step by step, and you will never be the same again!)

By now, you would have learnt that there are many pathways you can take to emerge from your 'cave', see things differently, and adapt yourself to living in the 'light'. But this is only the beginning! So get ready for an expansive, startling shift that will take you to a higher level…

View Corporate life not as Hunger games but as Contact sports

In conclusion, I want to urge that you view our life at work, not as a battle where we fight to the finish but as a pleasurable game where we may often play rough and tumble. The rules of the game often allow the occasional hurt and pain but there is an element of pleasure caused by the pain. Paradoxical it may seem, without being able to play with others, you may achieve the solo performance but true success is always based on a collaborative effort where a group feels that they contributed to the venture.

As long as we keep the view, that our work is not the defining factor, that we don't have to exterminate the other party, we can keep moving forward. In life, we needed a doctor, a mid-wife and a support team to bring us into this world, and we will probably need an undertaker and his team to let us down. Let us always bear in mind, that we will need to work alongside others and we need cheer leaders as well as contributors to our success.

Afterword

The Prisoner's Dilemma

Raj and Srinu have been arrested for robbing the Hibernia Savings Bank and placed in separate isolation cells. Both care much more about their personal freedom than about the welfare of their accomplice. A clever prosecutor makes the following offer to each. "You may choose to confess or remain silent. If you confess and your accomplice remains silent I will drop all charges against you and use your testimony to ensure that your accomplice does serious time. Likewise, if your accomplice confesses while you remain silent, he will go free while you do the time. If you both confess I get two convictions, but I'll see to it that you both get early parole. If you both remain silent, I'll have to settle for token sentences on firearms possession charges. If you wish to confess, you must leave a note with the jailer before my return tomorrow morning."

The "dilemma" faced by the prisoners here is that, whatever the other does, each is better off confessing than remaining silent. But the outcome obtained when both confess is worse for each than the outcome they would have obtained had both remained silent. A common view is that the puzzle illustrates a conflict between individual and group rationality. A group whose members pursue rational self-interest may all end up worse off than a group whose members act contrary to rational self-interest. More generally, if the payoffs are not assumed to represent self-interest, a group whose members rationally pursue any goals may all meet less success than if they had not rationally pursued their goals individually. A closely related view is that the prisoner's dilemma game and its multi-player generalizations model familiar situations in which it is difficult to get rational, selfish agents to cooperate for their common good.

To be successful is the mark of a life well lived, a race run well. But success can never be achieved in a vacuum, it always happens in the context of a corporate or a relational setting. Just like the Prisoner's dilemma, every executive invariably confronts is 'How much should I give before I start receiving?' What if I take a risk of trusting someone and I'm ripped off ? What if I bet it all on these paradigms and I am exploited?

After all, I may argue that I am not volunteering in a charity where the pay - off is not monetary but of satisfaction in lieu of currency. Such a basic question determines whether an employee is operating at the optimum best or cautiously playing well below potential. Such dilemmas determine whether all team members are performing at full throttle or there are others who freeloading at the expense of others who are driving hard. It is a pivotal question that sets the tone and tenor of the culture and success of organisations, teams and groups which individuals need to answer before they give it all, their time, talents, and undiluted fervour.

There is certainly that element of risk whenever you step out in faith. But here is the pay-off even when they try to take advantage of you. You played by your own rules and that is good enough to give you the high. You are not just on a higher ground by virtue of having a clean conscience, but you know that you've run your race well. If the man in the mirror thinks he won, then you don't need any other endorsement.

Tennyson said it best,
'I hold it true, whate'er befall;
I feel it, when I sorrow most;
'Tis better to have loved and lost
Than never to have loved at all.'

What does it take to give it your all?

Sunil Robert's debut book I Will Survive was a best-seller endorsed by global leaders, and resonated powerfully with India's burgeoning workforce. He now shares his wisdom in practical, real-life scenarios that are bound to challenge accepted norms of corporate life.

Corporate life is tough. Really tough. If the hours or the jargon ('think out of the box', bottomline, topline et al) don't get you, the politics most certainly will. Given that much of our waking hours are spent at work, how then does one negotiate the minefield that is the office? How does one get a life and also understand that we are much more than our jobs?

Enter Sunil Robert's 'Bound to Rise'. Its homespun wisdom and practical advice embellished with a number of real-life anecdotes shows you the way. Years of experience in varied sectors, job profiles and countries have given Sunil a unique view of corporate life. This view has been further enriched by his hobbies—sports writing and marathon running. All of this combine in giving the reader a fresh insight that enables him not just to survive, but 'TO RISE'.